To the apple of my eye, Thomas.
Without your support,
this book would not have been possible.

# An Invitation

# to the GARDEN

## SEASONAL ENTERTAINING OUTDOORS

Michael Devine

Foreword by
CHARLOTTE MOSS

Photography by
MICHAEL DEVINE and JOHN GRUEN

**RIZZOLI**
NEW YORK

New York Paris London Milan

# Contents

# Foreword

BY CHARLOTTE MOSS

orothy Draper said, "Entertaining is fun!" and titled her book the same. Elsa Maxwell, a professional hostess, wrote a book called *How To Do It or The Lively Art of Entertaining*. Both of these ladies wrote based on their experience as hostesses, and most importantly, on their respective philosophies of living the good life, specifically a life spent in the company of friends. In the book you are now holding, you can further your entertaining interests, be inspired by beautifully set tables, and encouraged to grab the chicest apron you own and give your Cuisinart a whirl.

Michael cooks all the food at his gatherings, and his recipes are the tried-and-true sort. While most people are scouring the local gourmet market in search of the perfect ingredients, or prepared and prepackaged morsels and delicacies, Michael is making selections from his own backyard garden. From his *jardin de curé*, a modern twist on the medieval cloister garden, he gathers herbs, flowers, and vegetables, all of which find their way to Michael's table. Some may end up in the pantry in the form of preserves and jams. Romantic names like Mara des Bois (strawberries), Comtesse de Chambord (rice beans), and Teton de Venus (tomatoes) add to the allure of an alfresco dinner and affect his selections in setting what is always a beautiful table. Every part of the process, from garden to table, has his hand in it—from the planning and planting, to cultivating, gathering, and cooking. And all of it takes place before the guests arrive.

Certainly a lot of detail goes into entertaining successfully, but one thing you can be sure of is that ease comes with practice, and all of that translates into fun for your guests. As I have been a guest at Michael's, I know firsthand that he has fun at his own parties. Whether he's hosting a five-course seated dinner or a casual tray-on-the-lap get-together, he is smiling as if someone else did all the work. He subscribes to Maxwell's philosophy that when the guests walk through the door, the party begins for everyone, host included.

In his enthusiastic greeting at the door, the festive decoration of the table, and the delicious menu, Michael's desire to delight his friends is on full display. Whether the settings are casual, with color scheme reflected in paper lanterns and bright zinnias, or more formal, with walls luxuriously draped in pagoda fabric and a mountain of lilacs on the table, one thing you can be sure of as Michael's guest: The atmosphere is one of "We're so glad you're here."

I am sure these entertaining stories will inspire you to experiment, encourage you to explore your cupboards in search of treasures long ignored, and, of course, have fun. Here, hospitality and exuberance meet daring and originality. RSVP to Michael's invitation to the garden, turn the page, and discover and delight in all things Devine.

Five must-have roses that were used for my Rose Pink Breakfast centerpiece: the delicate, sensual Mme Caroline de Testout, named after a fashionable nineteenth-century French couturiere; the deep velvety purple Cardinal de Richelieu; the Baronne Prévost, which blooms throughout the summer; the intense re-blooming Rose de Rescht; and the Pierre de Ronsard, with its elegant pale pink edges.

# Introduction

I grew up in a small village in the Midwest, where gardening, good food, and entertaining were the main pastimes. From a young age I helped with the planting and upkeep of my family's garden. The entire seasonal process of growing and preparing food became a vital rhythm in my life. With the freshest produce at our fingertips, memorable meals were created for family and friends. This was the nurturing and creative atmosphere that stimulated my enduring passion. In an environment like this, learning to cook was part and parcel of the way we lived.

As a youngster, I loved nothing more than polishing silver with my grandmother and hearing tales of long-ago parties that were still vivid in her memory. This thoughtful upbringing gave me the foundation to fuel my own style.

After college I moved to New York City and then to Paris, where I studied at the Sorbonne and the Ecole du Louvre, experiencing the city's highly influential *art de vivre*. Impressed with the amazing Parisian culinary scene, I took cooking courses at the Ritz Escoffier. I was also inspired by the unforgettable meals given by my French friends and their families. When I returned to New York, I became an editor and launched my hand-printed-fabric company as a creative sideline. Always knowing that I was destined for a rural environment like the one I'd grown up in, I eventually arrived in the historic village of Kinderhook in the Hudson River Valley, where I have spent the last eight years honing my skills as a cook, gardener, and host with my partner, Thomas.

When I bought my small property, the backyard was woefully in shambles, but with some imagination and lots of elbow grease, I transformed it into an elegant haven for all the senses. For the garden design, I was inspired by the French *jardin de curé* (priest's garden), where the priests grew flowers for decoration, fruits and vegetables for eating, and herbs for remedies. My garden is the raison d'être for breakfasts, lunches, drinks parties, and dinners that I host throughout the year. It provides fresh, organic produce for the dishes I prepare, and sensuous flowers of all shapes, sizes, and colors for a festive tabletop.

Each January, I look forward to the arrival of my order of seed packets. It never fails to amaze me that an entire year's harvest will grow from such small packages. Fresh ingredients are essential to making the most delicious meals, and what could be tastier than just-picked vegetables, herbs, and fruits? The food that I grow is the backbone of all the dishes that I prepare throughout the seasons. In the spring, the first salad greens poke through the soil, and the summer months provide a cornucopia of vegetables, berries, flowers, and herbs. Autumn

A mix of old and new tableware creates an enticing tablescape.

brings an abundance of potatoes, carrots, and tender spinaches. Even in the midst of winter's cold winds, leeks, celeriac, turnips, and Brussels sprouts thrive.

The meals that I love to cook are influenced by my love for France and the care the French take in even the smallest details. Menus should not be too complicated; they should be delicious and presented with flair. When I entertain, I lean on the classics—satisfying starters, filling main courses, and decadent desserts. And whenever I can, I throw parties inside the cozy bagatelle, an old garden shed that has been transformed into a whimsical dining space, in the back of the garden. Using my printed fabrics, creative centerpieces, the dinnerware I've collected, and other accents to set the *mise-en-scène*, I can tailor my outdoor entertaining to any occasion—from a butterfly-themed spring luncheon surrounded by lush plantings to an elegant Christmas Eve dinner in the bagatelle.

My garden is the place where I let my imagination run free. Welcome to my private Eden. I hope you enjoy this tour of my seasonal parties, and that they will inspire you to create enchanting events of your own.

Buffets are an easy way to entertain friends. OPPOSITE: Oeufs en Cocotte served with a salad make a filling main course for a simple buffet dinner. ABOVE: An enchanting seating area in the garden. The terrace floor is covered with pea stones similar to those found in the French countryside. OVERLEAF: My summer garden is a luxurious oasis of green with an exclamation point of pink geraniums and blue petunias in the center urn.

"The view of my little garden and the cheerful appearance of my studio always make me happy."

—EUGÈNE DELACROIX

# Lilac Brunch

Spring Sorrel and Salmon Tart

· ◆ ·

Green Salad with Light Vinaigrette

· ◆ ·

Strawberry Mille-Feuilles

· ◆ ·

Thyme Tea

· ◆ ·

Lilac-infused Water

· ◆ ·

Montrachet Blanc

# T

**HERE'S NOTHING QUITE LIKE THE EXCITEMENT**
of the first spring meal in the garden. By the time the lilacs have blossomed, the moment has come to start enjoying the garden, and I cannot think of a better way than with a brunch inspired by these fragrant, voluptuous blooms.

Lilacs are traditionally associated with first loves; so it's no wonder that they were the first flower I fell in love with during my childhood. They remind me of the house I grew up in, where a long stand of ancient lilacs brightened the backyard in hues of dark and light purple. Their heady scent used to fill the air on warm spring nights and was positively enchanting.

The lilac is my favorite harbinger of the season. In my eyes, spring hasn't arrived until the lilacs are in full bloom. They indicate that the threat of frost has passed and it's safe to start setting out cold-sensitive plants and entertain guests outside.

I am partial to the ease of Sunday brunches in the country. Friends often come over around eleven and have time to relax, enjoy a good meal and conversation, and still have most of the day afterward to do other things. Since this was a lilac-themed brunch, I waited until my two lilac bushes were going to be in bloom. Lilacs generally last a week to ten days, so there's a brief window of opportunity to invite a few friends over to enjoy the queen of the season.

For this special occasion, I decided to commemorate the lilac's Asian heritage. I thought it seemed fitting to turn the bagatelle—a garden shed refurbished in the spirit of French fantasy architecture—into an ode to all things chinoiserie. I love the walls to be hung with fabric—it's so unexpected and adds fantasy to the interior. I chose my fanciful pagoda fabric "Garden Folly," which matched the lighthearted mood I wanted to create. I printed the pattern in a bright fuchsia on crisp white to set off the color of the flowers, and stapled it to the walls.

The centerpiece needed to be a lush ode to the lilac. Vases were tightly packed with bunches of lilacs that I had preserved the night before in almost-boiling water. White porcelain monkeys from Mottahedeh added unexpected humor, snuggled into the great masses of lilacs. My custom service of eight hand-painted Limoges dinnerware settings by French designer Marie Daâge is decorated with enchanting monkeys and pagodas.

One of my fundamental rules for entertaining is to keep it simple, especially when cooking for a group. My menus are always based on what is available in the garden at the time. For this brunch, I had a lot of fresh lemony sorrel, crisp early lettuce, chives, mint, and rhubarb. Everything could be made or prepped before the guests arrived, and so when it came time to serve, the only thing I had to do was dress the salad and plate the food.

OPPOSITE: For this brunch in the bagatelle, I used hand-painted dinnerware by Marie Daâge and a tablecloth made from my "Pinwheel" fabric in pearl. OVERLEAF, LEFT: A porcelain monkey playing a flute coordinates with the monkeys on the cups. Inverted box-pleat curtains were made from my "Garden Folly" fabric, which was printed in a vibrant fuchsia to complement the lilacs. An aubergine grosgrain ribbon finishes the edges. OVERLEAF, RIGHT (clockwise from top left): Silver pagoda-shaped salt and peppers continue the chinoiserie theme. The centerpiece is a veritable forest of lilacs. Vintage damask napkins can be found for a song. For the party, I updated mine using lavender Rit dye. The pitcher of lilac-infused water is perfect for such an occasion.

## THYME TEA

This tea is a delightful and refreshing drink for the end of any meal. I use lemon thyme, but you should feel free to experiment with different varieties, since the thyme family is a large one and includes many flavors.

6 cups water
7 sprigs fresh lemon thyme
2 lemon slices
Honey or raw sugar, for serving

In a 2-quart saucepan, bring the water to a boil over high heat. Remove the pan from the heat and add the thyme and lemon slices; cover the pan and let the mixture infuse for 6 minutes. Strain the tea, and pour it into a teapot. Serve with honey or raw sugar. *Serves 6*

## LILAC-INFUSED
## WATER *(See page 19.)*

Add a handful of washed lilac blooms to a pitcher of cool water. Let it infuse for 6 to 12 hours before serving for a beautiful and refreshing flavored water. *Serves 6*

LEFT: The bagatelle in spring splendor.

## TIPS

There is no need to hammer the stems to make the lilacs perky. To keep them fresh longer, fill the vase with water that is just below the boiling point.

When transplanting seedlings, be sure to soak their roots in water before removing them from the container and planting them in the garden. It helps to ease this tricky transition.

When planting seeds that have a hard shell such as morning glories, peas, and nasturtiums—it's a good idea to soak them in room-temperature water overnight before planting.

ABOVE: Fresh lettuces waiting to be made into a salad to accompany the Spring Sorrel and Salmon Tart.
OPPOSITE: Lilacs in bloom in the garden.

# Spring Sorrel and Salmon Tart

*Serves 6*

Sorrel has a wonderful lemony flavor, which is a good complement to salmon. However, when cooked its color changes to a drab green, and so I like to add spinach for some extra color.

Preheat the oven to 350°F.

Line a 9-inch tart pan with a removable bottom with the pastry, and prick it all over with the tines of a fork. Bake for 12 minutes. Remove from the oven and set aside. Leave the oven on.

In a large skillet, melt the butter over medium-low heat. Add the shallot and cook for 5 minutes, or until it is translucent but not browned, stirring occasionally. Add the spinach and sorrel to the pan in small batches until all of it has wilted, 5 to 7 minutes. Remove the pan from the heat and set aside.

In a small bowl, mix together the eggs and crème fraîche; season to taste with salt and white pepper.

Transfer the spinach-sorrel mixture to the pastry shell. Scatter the cubed salmon evenly on top of the greens, and then spread the crème fraîche mixture over the top.

Bake the tart for 40 to 50 minutes, until it is set and golden brown on top. Remove the tart from the oven, cut it into wedges, and serve immediately with sprigs of dill.

1 sheet puff pastry, thawed if frozen

2 tablespoons unsalted butter

1 shallot, minced

8 ounces spinach, well washed and dried, stems removed

8 ounces sorrel, well washed and dried, stems removed

2 large eggs

¾ cup crème fraîche or sour cream

Sea salt

Freshly ground white pepper

8 ounces Atlantic salmon fillet, cut into ½-inch cubes

Small bunch of fresh dill, for garnish

# Green Salad with Light Vinaigrette

*Serves 6 to 8*

I like a very light vinaigrette on my salads, especially in the springtime. This recipe cuts the oil down by a third, for a lighter version of the classic.

Put the greens in a large serving bowl. Cover with plastic wrap, and refrigerate until ready to serve.

To make the vinaigrette: In a glass jar with a lid, combine the vinegar and salt. Seal the jar and shake vigorously to mix. Add the water, oil, mustard, and pepper, seal the jar, and shake again until thoroughly combined.

Just before serving, pour the vinaigrette over the chilled salad greens and toss to combine.

**OPTIONAL:** Garnish the salad with ¼ cup fresh lilac blossoms, rinsed and dried.

12 ounces assorted spring greens, well washed and dried, stems removed

1 tablespoon tarragon-flavored white wine vinegar

¼ teaspoon sea salt

1 tablespoon water

2 tablespoons extra-virgin olive oil

1 teaspoon Dijon mustard

¼ teaspoon freshly ground black pepper

# Strawberry Mille-Feuilles

*Serves 8*

These little delights are best when made with the freshest berries available. The lemon in the tuiles beautifully complements the tang of the crème fraîche.

### VANILLA CRÈME FRAÎCHE

In the bowl of a stand mixer fitted with the whisk attachment, whip the crème fraîche until stiff peaks form. Add the vanilla and sugar, and mix until thoroughly incorporated. Cover with plastic wrap, and refrigerate until ready to use.

### TUILES

In the bowl of a stand mixer fitted with the paddle attachment, cream together the butter and confectioners' sugar until the mixture is light and fluffy. Add the eggs one at a time, mixing well after each addition, and then add the flour, lemon zest, and lemon juice. Mix well to combine. Cover the bowl with plastic wrap, and refrigerate until well chilled, at least 1 hour to overnight.

Arrange racks in the top and bottom thirds of the oven, and preheat to 400°F. Line two baking sheets with parchment paper.

Using a pastry bag with a ½-inch round tip, pipe twelve mounds of tuile dough onto each prepared baking sheet, spacing the mounds about 3 inches apart.

With a teaspoon dipped in cold water, spread each mound of dough into a rectangle about 1½ by 3½ inches, leaving 2 inches of space between each one. Sprinkle each rectangle with a few almonds. Bake the tuiles for 10 to 12 minutes, or until the edges are brown and the centers are still pale. Remove the baking sheets from the oven and transfer the tuiles to a wire rack to cool completely.

### ASSEMBLE THE MILLE-FEUILLES

Neatly arrange eight strawberry halves on top of one tuile. Using a pastry bag fitted with a ½-inch star tip, pipe three rosettes of the crème fraîche along the center of the strawberry-covered tuile. Cover with another tuile, pressing it down gently, and cover that tuile with eight strawberry halves and three rosettes of crème fraîche. Cover with one more tuile, pressing down gently, and dust the top of the tuile with confectioners' sugar. Repeat with the remaining tuiles, strawberries, crème fraîche, and confectioners' sugar.

**OPTIONAL:** Garnish each mille-feuille with a little finely grated lemon zest.

---

### VANILLA CRÈME FRAÎCHE

8 ounces crème fraîche

½ teaspoon vanilla extract

¼ cup of granulated sugar

### TUILES

11 tablespoons unsalted butter at room temperature

¾ cup sifted confectioners' sugar, plus more for dusting

4 large eggs, at room temperature

⅔ cup cake flour

Grated zest of 1 organic lemon

1 teaspoon freshly squeezed lemon juice

1 cup slivered almonds

1 quart strawberries, rinsed, hulled, dried, and sliced in half lengthwise

# Rose Pink Breakfast

*Strawberries with Rose Water Syrup*

· ◆ ·

*Scrambled Eggs with Rose Petals
and Honey-Glazed Bacon*

· ◆ ·

*Rhubarb Muffins*

· ◆ ·

*Freshly Squeezed Orange Juice
and Coffee*

S THERE ANY FLOWER THAT CAN CONJURE SO MANY images and ideas as the rose? When I was laying out my garden, I was determined to put in as many roses as I could fit. I have about twenty-seven varieties, and most of them are heirlooms. The list of names of these flowers reads like the *Bottin mondain*. There's La Reine des Violettes, Cardinal de Richelieu, Mme Caroline de Testout, and Pierre de Ronsard, to name just a few.

Early June is when roses are at their peak, creating a kaleidoscope of pink, purple, and white throughout the garden. And while they provide a summer's worth of fragrant blooms in the garden and throughout the house, roses are also edible and offer culinary inspiration.

Some early June weekend houseguests provided the excuse for this intimate breakfast for four. The color concept was shades of pink with an accent of turquoise. I used a round table dressed with a tablecloth in my "Petite Fleur" print, a subtle pattern in cream on white. This created a neutral background for the rose centerpiece.

The centerpiece structure was made from several vintage pressed-glass compotes, which were stacked and then fitted together with scrunched-up chicken wire held in place with florist's tape. The chicken wire acted as a brace to hold the flowers. For the arrangement, I used a medley of about three dozen roses. Small bud vases were positioned at each place setting to show off individual blooms of my prized Cardinal de Richelieu and Rose de Rescht varieties.

The china was a mix of flea-market finds. The ivory- and gold-banded plates came from a nearby antiques store. They have a wonderful tortoised pattern in the glaze that only comes from age and use. The charming turquoise cups and saucers are from a Paris flea market and make an ideal breakfast service. For juice glasses, I used stemware with a pretty shape. My great-grandmother's silver elegantly tied everything together.

By early June the garden is taking off as the days get longer and warmer. The first of the bounty is coming to fruition. Fortunately, two of my favorite summer treats—raspberries and strawberries—have ever-bearing varieties. Once established, the plants are relatively carefree and provide an abundance of fruit throughout the summer and until the first frost. The Heritage raspberry and the Mara des Bois strawberry are amazing in tarts and ice cream.

The breakfast began with Mara des Bois strawberries paired with a rose water–flavored simple syrup. For the main course, I scrambled organic, free-range eggs and topped them with rose petals. Nothing compares to these delicious eggs with their rich yellow yolks. The eggs were accompanied by crisp, locally made bacon, artisanal pastries from the farmers' market, and homemade rhubarb muffins. It was a fitting start to a busy weekend.

OPPOSITE: An early-summer morning is the perfect occasion for breakfast in the garden. OVERLEAF, LEFT: To coordinate with the pinks in the rose arrangement, I set the table with delicately folded pale-pink napkins. OVERLEAF, RIGHT (clockwise from top left): Vintage sterling flatware and turquoise and white porcelain are cheerful accents to the roses. Mara des Bois strawberries, topped with rose petals, are served in etched glass compotes. The art of napkin folding is easy to master and adds much to a table setting. Surrounding the centerpiece are bud vases filled with alternating blooms of intense pink Rose de Rescht and deep, velvety purple Cardinal de Richelieu.

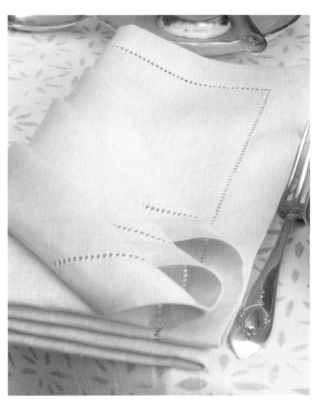

## TIPS

🌸 Rose season never has to end if you dry the petals of favorite roses and make your own potpourri.

🌸 I always use Epsom salts in the spring and mid-summer to give my plants—especially the roses—a boost. About 2 tablespoons per foot of planting will help them grow greener and be more productive.

🌸 When making an arrangement, be sure to trim off all the leaves so there are none in the water. If they are submerged in water, the leaves will begin to rot, causing a rank odor and fostering bacteria that can kill the bouquet.

ABOVE: Roses and their petals floating in my fountain. OPPOSITE: One of the most gorgeous moments in the garden is when the Pierre de Ronsard roses are in full bloom and cascade down the length of the fence.

# Strawberries with Rose Water Syrup

*Serves 4*

Rose water adds an unexpected flavor to the already heady aroma of perfectly ripe strawberries. Be sure to trim the white edges from the rose petals, though, as they can be very bitter. *(See page 33.)*

Combine the sugar and rose water in a large glass bowl. Add the strawberries and toss to coat. Cover the bowl and refrigerate the berries for 6 hours, stirring occasionally.

Divide the berries among 4 serving dishes. Sprinkle with rose petals and serve.

3 tablespoons granulated sugar

2 tablespoons rose water

1 pint strawberries, rinsed, hulled, and sliced

Assorted organically grown rose petals, rinsed, white parts trimmed and discarded

# Scrambled Eggs with Rose Petals and Honey-Glazed Bacon

*Serves 4*

When I make scrambled eggs I count two eggs per person, plus one extra. As for cooking time, it's a matter of taste; I prefer mine soft and a little wet, but if you like yours harder and on the dry side, keep cooking for a few minutes longer. Honey-glazed bacon is a flavorful alternative to standard bacon.

### SCRAMBLED EGGS
Break the eggs into a large mixing bowl, and whisk them together with the water until they are uniform in color. Season to taste with salt and white pepper.

In a large nonstick skillet, melt the butter over medium-low heat. Pour the eggs into the pan and cook, stirring constantly, until they reach your desired consistency. (For soft, slightly wet scrambled eggs, cook them for 3 to 4 minutes.)

Sprinkle the rose petals over top and serve immediately.

### HONEY-GLAZED BACON
Preheat the oven to 375°F. Line a rimmed baking sheet with parchment paper.

Neatly lay the bacon strips in a single layer on the prepared baking sheet. Brush the honey on the top of the bacon to coat.

Bake the bacon for 20 to 25 minutes, until browned. Using tongs or a spatula, transfer the bacon to paper towels to drain for a moment, then serve hot.

### SCRAMBLED EGGS

9 large eggs

2 teaspoons water

Fine sea salt

Freshly ground white pepper

1½ tablespoons unsalted butter

Assorted organically grown rose petals, rinsed, white parts trimmed and discarded

### HONEY-GLAZED BACON

1 pound thick-cut bacon (about 3 slices per person)

⅓ cup honey, warmed

# Rhubarb Muffins

*Makes 18 muffins*

These muffins are an easy and quick breakfast treat. Using fresh rhubarb from the garden and topping them with pecans and granulated sugar will make the muffins all the more tantalizing.

Preheat the oven to 350°F. Spray 1½ standard muffin tins (18 cups) with nonstick cooking spray, or line the cups with cupcake liners, and set aside.

In a large bowl, whisk together the all-purpose flour, cake flour, 1 cup of the sugar, the baking powder, and salt, and set aside.

In a separate bowl, whisk together the eggs, oil, sour cream, and vanilla until smooth. Pour the egg mixture into the flour mixture and stir with a wooden spoon or silicone spatula to combine. Add the rhubarb and fold it into the batter until fully incorporated.

Make the topping: In a small bowl, toss together the pecans and the remaining ¼ cup sugar.

Spoon the batter into the prepared cups, filling each halfway, then sprinkle each with about 2 teaspoons of the pecan mixture.

Bake for 20 to 25 minutes, until the muffins are light golden brown and spring back to the touch. Remove the pan from the oven, and carefully transfer the muffins to a rack to cool completely before serving.

Cooking spray

1½ cups all-purpose flour

½ cup cake flour

1¼ cups granulated sugar

¾ teaspoon baking powder

½ teaspoon salt

2 large eggs

¾ cup vegetable oil

½ cup sour cream

1 teaspoon vanilla extract

1 cup finely chopped rhubarb

⅓ cup finely chopped pecans

# Light Lobster Lunch

*Homemade Lemon Soda*

• ◆ •

*Chilled Terrine of Summer Vegetables*

• ◆ •

*Lobsters Poached in Court Bouillon*

• ◆ •

*Raspberry Sorbet with*
*Chocolate-Dipped Mint Leaves*

• ◆ •

*Chilled Chablis*

Y FAVORITE COLOR COMBINATION FOR SUMMER
is classic blue and white. The cool crispness of the contrast makes it a natural for summer
entertaining and sets the tone for our annual Lobster Lunch in the Garden, a casual, relaxed
get-together with a few of our good friends in the neighborhood.

For this year's Lobster Lunch in mid-June, I made a centerpiece bursting with bachelor's
buttons in a marvelous basket hand-painted by Roger Banks-Pye, a noted decorator at the
Colefax & Fowler decorating firm for years and one of the most creative and elegant men in
design during his lifetime. I was fortunate enough to have received this basket as a gift from
one of his close friends. The simplicity of the centerpiece basket seemed to beckon an equally
simple flower, which is why I chose the blue bachelor's buttons, which also hold up well in the
heat of the day.

Building on the blue and white theme, I chose my crisp "Pavilion Stripe" tablecloth in
indigo and delft on white and added coral as the accent color. I was also lucky enough to
find lobster salt and pepper shakers to accentuate the lunch's crustacean theme. The addition
of coral fragments and beaded Dransfield & Ross napkin rings combined well with napkins
made from my whimsical "Pinwheel" fabric in coral and white. For flatware, I went with natural
bamboo, which I think goes with just about any type of country table setting.

When my guests arrived, I was ready to serve them wonderful homemade lemon soda.
I made it using the Meyer lemons that happened to have ripened just in time for the get-
together. The lemon syrup for the soda is a great make-ahead item. It can be mixed with seltzer
for a cool, refreshing nonalcoholic drink, or with vodka for a headier concoction.

The starter was a terrine of flavorful summer vegetables that had ripened early due to an
exceptionally warm spring that year. The star of the day, fresh-caught lobster, was served solo
with hearty peasant bread and individual containers of melted butter. I love to cook lobster in
a savory court bouillon of white wine and bouquet garni, which adds a wonderful flavor to an
already delectable treat.

Dessert was a simple homemade raspberry sorbet served with chocolate-dipped mint
leaves. For an extra-chocolatey flavor, I used the leaves from the chocolate mint plant. Mints
come in a wide variety of specialty flavors well beyond the common peppermint and spearmint
varieties; I grow pineapple, chocolate, apple, and orange, to name a few.

OPPOSITE: Looking in from the garden gate, the blue and white–themed table is a welcoming sight. OVERLEAF, LEFT: Lobster salt and pepper shakers mix with coral accessories and blue Murano swirl glasses. For the center of the table, a painted wooden apple basket was filled with bachelor's buttons. OVERLEAF, RIGHT (clockwise from top): The beaded coral napkin ring looks smashing with a napkin made from my coral "Pinwheel" fabric. The flatware has real bamboo handles. The lobster shakers are a whimsical touch. White bud vases filled with bachelor's buttons surround the centerpiece.

ABOVE, LEFT: My Sneeboer spade
is a favorite gardening tool.
ABOVE, RIGHT: One of my favorite
annuals, the charming bachelor's
button, which grows wild in fields,
is also known as the cornflower.
It symbolizes fidelity and hope.
OPPOSITE: The seating area's
Chinese garden stool functions as
a decorative drinks table.

## TIPS

❧ It's never too early to start thinking about the fall/winter garden. Do you have
all the seeds you need to plant? Are there seedlings that need to be started?

❧ Dead-head your plants to keep the flowers blooming all summer long.

❧ A warmed hand towel that has been heated with fresh sage leaves is an elegant
way for guests to clean their hands after eating deliciously messy lobster.

# Homemade Lemon Soda

*Makes 10 to 12 servings*

I love making my own drink mixes. Knowing exactly what they were concocted with is a major benefit that I find only enhances the pleasure of the elixir. Make the lemon syrup a day ahead so it has time to infuse.

Put the sugar in a nonreactive 2-quart saucepan. Using a micro-grater, grate the rind of the lemons onto the sugar. Cut the lemons in half and squeeze the juice into a measuring cup. Strain the juice through a fine-mesh sieve into the sugar-zest mixture. Add the water to the pan and stir to combine.

Place the pan over medium-high heat and bring to a rolling boil, stirring occasionally. When the mixture boils, remove the pan from the heat and let the syrup cool to room temperature. Pour it into a medium glass bowl. Cover and refrigerate the syrup overnight.

Before serving, remove the syrup from the refrigerator and strain it into a pretty serving carafe. For each soda, fill a glass with ice, add 3 tablespoons of the lemon syrup, and top it off with seltzer. Garnish with mint leaves and lemon slices.

**NOTE:** The lemon syrup will keep for 2 to 3 days, covered in the refrigerator.

2 cups superfine sugar

5 organic lemons, washed and dried

¾ cup water

2 liters seltzer

Fresh mint leaves and lemon slices, for garnish

# Chilled Terrine of Summer Vegetables

*Serves 6 to 8*

This is a wonderful starter that is best made the day before. It is also a great recipe for some of the garden's most abundant summer occupants.

Line a 9-by-5-inch loaf pan with parchment paper, leaving a 4-inch overhang on all sides. Line two broiler pans or baking sheets with foil.

Preheat the broiler to high.

Pour ¼ cup of the olive oil into a small bowl. Brush the peppers with the oil and place them on a lined broiler pan. Broil for 5 to 10 minutes, until the skin is blackened and begins to flake. Remove the pan from the broiler and let the peppers cool slightly, then peel off the skins and set the peppers aside.

Brush both sides of the zucchini and eggplant slices with oil and place them on a clean, lined broiler pan. Broil for 3 minutes on each side, or until the vegetables are tender. Remove the pan from the broiler and set the vegetable slices aside on paper towels to drain.

In a food processor fitted with a blade, pulse the goat cheese, season with the salt and white pepper to taste, and drizzle in the remaining 3 tablespoons of oil. Pulse until smooth and creamy.

In the prepared loaf pan, arrange zucchini strips lengthwise in a single layer, trimming as necessary to fit.

Spread one-third of the goat cheese mixture evenly over the zucchini layer. Arrange one-third of the eggplant strips in a single layer on top of the goat cheese, and top that with a layer of basil leaves. Next, scatter one-third of the sun-dried tomatoes on top of the basil. Repeat these layers two more times, ending with the pepper layer. Gently press down on the terrine to merge the layers and cover it with the overhanging parchment paper. Refrigerate the terrine for 6 to 24 hours. Unwrap, invert onto a platter or cutting board, remove the paper, slice, and serve.

¼ cup plus 3 tablespoons extra-virgin olive oil

2 red bell peppers, washed and quartered, seeds removed

2 medium zucchini, washed and cut lengthwise into ¼-inch-thick slices

1 large eggplant, washed and cut lengthwise into ¼-inch-thick slices

1 (11-ounce) package soft goat cheese

¼ teaspoon sea salt

Freshly ground white pepper

1 bunch fresh basil, washed and dried, stemmed

1 (8-ounce) jar sun-dried tomatoes in oil

# Lobsters Poached in Court Bouillon

*Serves 6*

This is my favorite way to prepare lobster; it takes a little more time than the traditional method of boiling, but it is well worth the effort. I always buy the smallest lobsters in the tank; I find that they are more tender than the larger ones.

In a large stewing pot over medium heat, combine the wine, water, the bouquet garni, salt, and peppercorns. Bring just barely to a boil, then cover the pot, reduce the heat to low, and let the mixture simmer for 25 minutes. Increase the heat to high, bring the bouillon to a rolling boil, and let it boil for 5 minutes. Add 2 lobsters to the boiling bouillon, headfirst. Cover the pot and cook until the lobsters are bright red, about 8 minutes. Remove the cooked lobsters from the pot and repeat with the remaining lobsters.

Serve the lobsters immediately with melted butter and country-style bread.

1 (750-ml) bottle of dry white wine

3¼ cups water

1 bouquet garni tied with string (recipe follows)

2 teaspoons coarse sea salt

1 teaspoon whole black peppercorns

6 (1- to 1¼-pound) freshly caught live lobsters

Melted unsalted butter and country-style bread, for serving

## BOUQUET GARNI

To make a bouquet garni, take one celery stalk (about 9 inches) and cut it in half. Fill each half with sprigs of fresh thyme and flat-leaf parsley and a bay leaf, and use kitchen twine to tie the halves together, sandwich-style, with the herbs in the center. Leave long tails of string when you tie the bouquet together, and use them to make a 4-inch loop that will help you to fish it out of the bouillon.

# Raspberry Sorbet with Chocolate-Dipped Mint Leaves

*Serves 6*

I use fresh raspberries from my garden to make this sorbet. It is equally delicious with good-quality frozen raspberries. A delightful addition to the sorbet is chocolate-dipped mint leaves, which contain raw egg whites. The chocolate mint variety, which I use in this recipe, is also wonderful as a tea, steeped in hot water and sweetened with raw sugar.

### SORBET

Freeze the bowl of your ice-cream maker a day ahead, if necessary (follow the manufacturer's instructions).

In a 1-quart saucepan over medium-high heat, combine the water and the sugar and bring to a rolling boil. Remove the pan from the heat, cover, and refrigerate for 2 hours, or until well chilled.

In a blender or food processor, puree the raspberries until smooth. I generally leave the seeds in the sorbet, but if you prefer your sorbet seed-free, use a nonreactive fine-mesh sieve to strain the raspberries until smooth. Pour the puree into a medium glass bowl, and place the glass bowl in a larger bowl filled with ice. Stir the puree with a rubber or silicone spatula until cool, 5 to 10 minutes.

Retrieve the chilled sugar syrup from the refrigerator and stir it into the raspberry puree, mixing well to combine. Pour the mixture into the ice-cream maker and make the sorbet according to the manufacturer's instructions.

### CHOCOLATE-DIPPED MINT LEAVES

Set a piece of waxed paper on a work surface. Line a tray or baking sheet with a clean piece of waxed paper.

Put the egg whites in a small bowl and beat with a fork to combine. Using a small food-safe paintbrush, brush the front and back of each mint leaf with the beaten egg whites, then quickly dredge in the sugar to coat each side. Set the sugar-coated leaves on the waxed paper as you work, and let them dry for about 20 minutes.

When the leaves are dry, melt the chocolate over low heat in the top of a double boiler, stirring constantly to avoid burning. Remove the pan from the heat and pour the chocolate into a small cup. Holding the stem end, dip the top half of each dried mint leaf into the chocolate to coat. Place the chocolate-coated leaves on the prepared tray. Cover the tray with plastic wrap and place it in the refrigerator for 3 hours to chill the leaves and set the chocolate.

### TO SERVE

Scoop the sorbet into ice-cream bowls and top with Chocolate-Dipped Mint Leaves.

---

**RASPBERRY SORBET**

1 cup water

1¼ cups granulated sugar

2 pounds raspberries, rinsed

**CHOCOLATE-DIPPED MINT LEAVES**

2 large egg whites

24 fresh chocolate mint leaves, washed and dried

3 tablespoons granulated sugar

4 ounces dark chocolate, coarsely chopped

# Lantern-Lit Drinks Party

*Savory Mini Muffins*

*Honey-Glazed Cherry Tomatoes*

*Tempura Fried Herbs*

*Feta Zucchini Rounds*

*Charcuterie*

*Orange-Chocolate Heart-shaped Brownies*

*Marshmallow Pops*

*San Pellegrino and Red and White Sancerre*

LOVE PARTIES. I LOVE GOING TO THEM AND I LOVE hosting them. For this summer-night get-together in the garden, I decided to create a colorful affair. The table's centerpiece was made from branches painted white and hung with inexpensive multicolored lanterns fitted with small reusable LED battery votives. The lanterns provided a vibrant burst of light to the table. The vase holding the branches was a dollar-store terra-cotta planter that I painted white and covered with inexpensive grosgrain ribbons that matched the lanterns. For heightened impact, I invited everyone to arrive after dark; walking into the candlelit garden toward the lantern arrangement was very dramatic and unexpected.

I served everything buffet style, which made entertaining relatively carefree once the party started. The food was served on an assortment of trays laminated with my fabrics in different colors, and the table was dressed in a perky yellow tablecloth. The red and white wines were kept in an ice bucket, which allowed the guests to serve themselves at their leisure. Maintaining the colorful theme of the evening, I opted for handy multicolored tapas plates and vibrant green napkins. Since the menu was all finger food, I didn't need to use flatware— another labor- and time-saving trick. The flowers were a vibrant assortment of fresh-cut zinnias from the garden. Their happy colors really brightened the table.

In my opinion, simple food that can be eaten while standing and chatting is a must for a cocktail party. Zucchini rounds with feta and chive mousse, a selection of beautiful crunchy Tempura Fried Herbs, and Savory Mini Muffins with goat cheese and red pepper were served along with a traditional French platter of charcuterie, cornichons, mustard, and olives.

Earlier that year when I had visited Paris, I was smitten with the novelty sweets in the windows of the patisseries. Beyond the usual array of traditional petits fours, there were revamped classics such as brownies and pops. For this party, I created chocolate-covered Marshmallow Pops and little heart-shaped brownies, based on ones I discovered in the Parisian pastry shop window displays.

On the night of the party, there was a clear sky full of stars and a brilliant full moon that bathed the garden in a beautiful poetic light. The central allée was lit by tole lanterns.

When planning the garden, I always make sure that there are enough white or light-colored flowers interspersed through the space. There is a simple reason for this: They stand out better in the dark with only moonlight and the glow of the lanterns. I am particularly partial to the "Jasmine" variety of nicotiana. It is a great flower for the evening garden, with white petals that stand out against the darkness and fragrant blooms that scent the garden.

# TIPS

🐝 I lay down the first thick layer of mulch around the beginning of July when the garden is almost filled in for the season. I have found that doing so earlier provides too much shelter for a variety of insects that feast on the tender seedlings.

🐝 Cherry tomatoes are one of my favorite garden plants. They start producing in mid-June and just keep going until the end of the summer.

🐝 Ice cubes made with multicolored bachelor's buttons keep wine cool, while adding a visual accent. Why not try nasturtiums, rose petals, or any other edible flower?

# Savory Mini Muffins

*Makes about 36*
*(Serves 12 to 14)*

The French often make savory cakes to serve with drinks, but for this party, I improvised and made mini muffins instead. They are much easier to eat standing up than a slice of cake! *(See Page 61.)*

Preheat the oven to 350°F.

In a small sauté pan, heat the olive oil over medium-low heat. Add the diced bell peppers and cook until tender, 5 to 7 minutes. Remove the pan from the heat and let the peppers cool to room temperature.

In a large glass bowl, using a wooden spoon, mix together the flour, baking powder, Gruyère, cooled peppers, nutmeg, salt, and white pepper until well blended. In a separate small bowl, whisk together the milk, sour cream, melted butter, and eggs until well blended. Add the milk mixture to the flour mixture, and stir until combined.

Divide the batter evenly among three non-stick 12-cup mini-muffin pans (or one and a half 24-cup mini-muffin pans). Bake for 25 minutes, or until the muffins spring back to the touch.

Let the muffins cool slightly before serving. Any extras can be stored in the freezer for up to two months.

2 tablespoons extra-virgin olive oil

1 green bell pepper, rinsed and diced

1 red bell pepper, rinsed and diced

1½ cups all-purpose flour

2 teaspoons baking powder

½ cup grated Gruyère cheese

¼ teaspoon ground nutmeg

½ teaspoon fine sea salt

¼ teaspoon freshly ground white pepper

½ cup whole milk

1 cup sour cream

⅓ cup unsalted butter, melted

3 eggs

# Honey-Glazed Cherry Tomatoes

*Makes 24*
*(Serves 12 to 14)*

These cocktail-party treats are a snap to make. Alternating yellow and red tomatoes create a checkerboard-like effect and complement other bright colors on a buffet table. *(See Page 61.)*

In a small saucepan over medium heat, combine the honey, sugar, and water; bring to a boil, stirring occasionally. When the mixture boils, remove the pan from the heat and let it cool to room temperature, about 20 minutes.

Insert a toothpick or small skewer into each tomato. Dip the tomatoes in the honey syrup to coat, then sprinkle the glazed tomatoes with flax seeds.

Serve immediately.

½ cup honey

½ cup granulated sugar

¼ cup water

24 cherry tomatoes, rinsed and dried

½ cup flax seeds

# Tempura Fried Herbs

*Makes 36*
*(Serves 12 to 14)*

Quickly frying herbs in a tempura batter makes a delicious and unusual treat to serve with drinks. The key to this recipe is keeping all of the ingredients as cold as possible. A simple piece of slate creates a dramatic surface.

Wrap the herbs in a barely damp paper towel and refrigerate them for 1 hour.

Prepare the tempura batter in a medium bowl according to the package directions. Set the bowl inside a larger bowl filled with ice to keep the batter chilled.

Fill a deep fryer with oil, about 1½ inches deep, and heat it according to the manufacturer's directions. Test the heat of the oil.

Dip each herb sprig into the batter and press lightly to coat; shake off the excess batter. Quickly fry the herbs for about 2 minutes, until golden. Remove the fried herbs from the hot oil with tongs and place them on paper towels to drain. Sprinkle with fleur de sel and serve immediately.

12 sprigs of three different varieties of herbs (such as basil, parsley, and sage, or thyme, rosemary, and tarragon), rinsed and thoroughly dried

1 package tempura mix

Canola oil, for frying

Fleur de sel

# Feta Zucchini Rounds

*Makes 24*
*(Serves 12)*

I count two pieces per person when I serve these along with a large assortment of different hors d'oeuvres. *(See Page 61.)*

In a medium glass bowl, using a wooden spoon, cream together the cheese and the oil until smooth. Add the shallot, minced chives, salt, white pepper, and cayenne and mix well to combine.

Using a piping bag fitted with a ½-inch star tip, pipe some creamed feta onto each zucchini round and place it on a serving platter. Sprinkle the remaining chives over the top.

Cover the platter with plastic wrap, and refrigerate until ready to serve. Serve cold.

12 ounces feta cheese

1½ tablespoons extra-virgin olive oil

1 shallot, minced

1 small bunch of fresh chives, washed and dried, 1 tablespoon very finely minced, the rest cut into 1¼-inch lengths

½ teaspoon fine sea salt

¼ teaspoon freshly ground white pepper

Dash of cayenne pepper

2 medium zucchini, washed and cut into 24 (¼-inch) rounds

# Charcuterie

*Makes about 36*
*(Serves 12 to 14)*

For a buffet, I serve a platter of cured meats bought from a gourmet grocery store. My three must-haves are sopressata, prosciutto di Parma, and a hard salami such as Genoa.

Serve the meats with sliced French baguette rounds set on a tray, crackers (Carr's Table Water and Cracked Pepper Crackers) and breadsticks (Grissini) in colorful containers, along with cornichons and whole grain mustard. Fill bowls with pitted oil-cured black olives and almonds topped with a sprig of rosemary. Add an artful display of seedless green and red grapes to the table.

Apportion 1 ounce cured meat per person.

# Orange-Chocolate Heart-shaped Brownies

*Makes 16 small brownies*

I made these brownies, with a subtle hint of orange, for the party in heart-shaped silicone muffin pans a day ahead. Using an atypically shaped baking pan is an easy way to add flair to this delicious dessert. In a pinch, you can use a great brownie mix such as Ghirardelli's. *(See Page 61.)*

Position a rack in the center of the oven and preheat to 350°F. Spray two heart-shaped muffin pans (each with 8-cavities) with nonstick cooking spray and set aside.

In the top of a double boiler, combine the butter and the chopped dark chocolate over low heat, stirring occasionally with a wooden spoon until the mixture is melted and smooth. Set aside to cool.

In a large bowl, whisk the eggs, then whisk in salt, sugar, and orange flower water until smooth. Stir in the chocolate mixture, then add the flour, orange zest, and chocolate chips and mix well with a wooden spoon or silicone spatula until fully incorporated.

Divide the batter evenly among the prepared heart-shaped cavities, filling each halfway. Bake for about 25 minutes, until the brownie tops have formed a shiny crust and the brownies are moderately firm. Let the brownies cool in the pans on a wire rack. Carefully unmold and store overnight in an airtight container in the refrigerator. Bring the brownies to room temperature before serving.

Cooking spray

1 cup (2 sticks) unsalted butter

5 ounces dark chocolate, cut into ¼-inch pieces

4 large eggs

¼ teaspoon fine sea salt

1½ cups granulated sugar

2 teaspoons orange flower water

¾ cup unbleached all-purpose flour

1 tablespoon finely grated orange zest

1 cup dark chocolate chips

# Marshmallow Pops

*Makes 24 (Serves 12 to 14)*

These s'mores-like pops add a sweet note to a table of savory foods. They are an unexpected treat for any occasion.

Insert a skewer into each marshmallow, and set aside. Put the graham crackers in a shallow bowl and place a sheet of waxed paper nearby on the counter.

In the top of a double boiler, melt the chocolate over low heat, stirring constantly to avoid burning. When all the chocolate has melted, remove the pan from the heat.

Working one at a time, dip the marshmallows first in chocolate, then in graham crackers to coat. Place the finished pops on the waxed paper to cool and set.

Leftover pops will keep for up to 3 days at room temperature in an airtight container.

24 artisanal vanilla marshmallows

1¼ cups coarsely crushed graham crackers

12 ounces dark chocolate, coarsely chopped

# Alfresco Evening Dinner

Chilled Zucchini Soup

*·◆·*

Thyme-Marinated Lamb  Chops

*·◆·*

Green Beans with
White Wine and Walnuts

*·◆·*

Vanilla Ice Milk with Gooseberry Sauce

*·◆·*

Chilled White Sancerre

OPPOSITE: The table set for an alfresco dinner. Gold ballroom chairs add extra sparkle to the green-and-blue color scheme. OVERLEAF, LEFT: The hydrangeas were flourishing in stunning shades of blue and lavender. Adding a couple of leaves to the blue hydrangea centerpiece provides subtle contrast. My collection of Japanese hand-painted figurines makes an amusing group for the table. OVERLEAF, RIGHT (clockwise from top left): Dessert served in etched coupe glasses. One figurine plays a little night song, while another pirouettes. Chilled zucchini soup garnished with parsley and a drizzle of olive oil.

THE TABLE SETTING FOR THIS MID-JULY DINNER was inspired by my passion for the whimsical hand-painted Meissen figurines of the eighteenth century. Though the real ones are far out of my price range, a few years ago I stumbled upon a group of more affordable and equally alluring substitutes at a ramshackle community-center sale. My motley crew of hand-painted figurines was actually produced as part of the economic reconstruction of Japan just after World War II, and their fetching colors and strong personalities immediately won me over. These cast-porcelain figurines each have their very own personality, and as a group they form a hilarious band that leads to great conversation.

The vibrant blue hydrangeas—blooming profusely at the time in my garden—were an ideal choice for the dinner table's centerpiece. Though they are majestic in color and in size, they are relatively fragrance-free, and therefore will not overpower guests with a battle of scents between the flowers and the food.

For the tablecloth, I used my "Charlotte" fabric in a beautiful yellowish green called absinthe to complement the hydrangeas and create a relatively neutral background for the colorful porcelain figurines (which we now refer to as the "hydrangea people"). I used beautiful American service plates with wide cerulean-blue bands to coordinate with the blue flowers and the green tablecloth. Since I wanted a more formal feel to the dinner, I rented gold bamboo ballroom chairs to enhance the sense of occasion.

By then there was a wealth of fresh, homegrown vegetables, herbs, and fruits to choose from for the menu. We started with rich and creamy zucchini soup that had a bit of zip from a sly addition of cayenne pepper. This soup is a particularly good choice because it uses a fair amount of zucchini and is served chilled, making it a no-fuss starter. The main course was lamb rib chops marinated in a thyme-infused marinade and served with green beans tossed with toasted walnuts in a white wine–butter sauce. I think green beans should always be picked when they are very young and at their tender best. Bottles of chilled Sancerre were at the ready. Dessert was a simple, luscious bowl of vanilla ice milk topped with a homemade gooseberry sauce made from homegrown gooseberries, and light, crisp store-bought cookies.

- At the beginning of the growing season and once again midseason, add a few tablespoons of sulfur to the hydrangeas to ensure a vivid blue color.

- Renting chairs, tables, and dinnerware is a great option if you don't have what you need on hand. It's much more reasonable than buying numerous items and having to find storage for things you may only use once, if ever, again.

- I used my collection of inexpensive Japanese-made figurines to create a memorable tablescape. Any amusing collection will do—the more unusual, the greater the impact.

LEFT: Setting the table is always easier if it is pre-planned to the last detail the day before or the morning of a party. Vintage cerulean service plates complement the hydrangea arrangement magnificently. OVERLEAF: The seating area is surrounded by glorious flowering plants. A planter of nicotiana in full bloom scents the warm night air with its rich fragrance.

# Chilled Zucchini Soup

Chilled soup is one of my favorite starters for a meal. It can be made a day ahead of time and kept in a sealed container in the refrigerator to thoroughly chill. By peeling the zucchini, you ensure that the soup won't turn bitter. A drizzle of olive oil and a sprig of parsley add the finishing touch. *(See page 75.)*

In a 5-quart stockpot, heat 2 tablespoons of oil over medium heat. Add the zucchini and garlic to the pot, and cook for 5 to 10 minutes, until tender. Stir in the stock, cayenne, and salt. Simmer for 20 minutes, and then remove the pot from the heat.

With an immersion blender, puree the soup in the pot until it is smooth and creamy. Alternatively, pour the soup into a food processor or blender, in batches if necessary, let cool for a few minutes, then puree until smooth. Adjust the seasonings to taste.

Transfer the soup to an airtight container and refrigerate for 4 to 6 hours.

When the soup has been thoroughly chilled, divide it among 8 individual bowls and drizzle some of the remaining 2 tablespoons of oil on top of each serving. Garnish with the parsley sprigs and serve.

4 tablespoons extra-virgin olive oil

6 medium zucchini, peeled and cubed

4 garlic cloves, crushed

2 cups vegetable stock

⅛ teaspoon cayenne pepper, or more if needed

½ teaspoon coarse sea salt, or more if needed

8 small sprigs flat-leaf parsley, for garnish

# Thyme-Marinated Lamb Chops

Always a crowd pleaser, these chops are great any time of the year.

In a small bowl, whisk together the oil, thyme, garlic, pepper, and salt. Place the lamb chops on a shallow platter large enough to hold all of them in a single layer, and pour the marinade over the top, turning the chops to coat them evenly. Cover the platter with plastic wrap and refrigerate the chops for 3 hours, turning them over halfway through.

Preheat an outdoor grill to medium-high. Grill the chops for 4 to 5 minutes on each side, or until an instant-read meat thermometer inserted in the center registers 160°F. Serve immediately.

½ cup extra-virgin olive oil

⅓ cup fresh thyme, finely chopped

3 garlic cloves, minced

Coarsely ground black pepper

Fine sea salt

16 lamb rib chops

# Green Beans with White Wine and Walnuts

*Serves 8*

These beans are tossed in a variation of beurre blanc that adds wonderful flavor. I prefer to use Comtesse de Chambord rice beans, but if they aren't available, haricots verts—either fresh or frozen—or regular string beans are fine substitutes. *(See page 81.)*

Place a fine-mesh sieve in a large serving bowl, and set aside next to the stove.

In a nonstick frying pan over medium heat, toast the walnuts until golden brown, 6 to 8 minutes. Remove from the heat and set aside.

In a medium saucepan, melt the butter over medium-low heat and add the shallot. Cook the shallot until tender, about 4 minutes, and then add the wine, salt, and pepper. Cook until the liquid is reduced by half, about another 5 minutes. Remove the pan from the heat and strain the sauce through the sieve into the large serving bowl. Cover the bowl with plastic wrap and set aside.

Fill a 5-quart saucepan halfway with water, and place the pan over medium-high heat. Bring the water to a rolling boil, and add the beans. Return the water to a boil, and cook the beans for 2 to 3 minutes, until just tender.

Immediately drain the beans and return them to the empty pan over medium heat. Toss the beans for 2 minutes to remove any excess moisture.

Add the beans to the wine sauce in the large serving bowl, and toss well. Adjust the seasonings to taste, add the toasted walnuts, and toss once more to combine. Serve immediately.

¾ cup chopped walnuts

4 tablespoons unsalted butter

1 shallot, minced

1¼ cups dry white wine

Fine sea salt

Coarsely ground pepper

1½ pounds green beans (preferably Comtesse de Chambord rice beans), ends removed

## BEANS

For years I favored the traditional French haricots verts, which are easily available. Now, I have moved on to the rare and almost ethereally delicate Comtesse de Chambord rice beans. These aristocratic beans are smaller than their cousin, the haricots verts, and because they are so precious, they are almost impossible to transport and never seen outside of the gardens they grew in. When in season, they need to be picked every two days.

# Vanilla Ice Milk with Gooseberry Sauce

*Serves 8*

I added gooseberries to the garden as a bit of a lark, and I am glad I did. They require nominal care and are bountiful producers once established. I like to make this dessert especially because the gooseberry sauce is an unusual treat for most people. I suggest for super-easy preparation, make the sauce a day ahead, freeze the ice milk or buy a gourmet ice cream, and serve with light, crisp cookies on the side. *(See page 75.)*

Combine the gooseberries, sugar, and water in a medium saucepan, and cook over medium heat until the berries are tender and reduced to a pulp, 10 to 15 minutes.

Remove the pan from the heat and strain through a fine-mesh sieve to strain the sauce into an airtight glass container. Cover the container, and let the sauce cool to room temperature, 20 to 25 minutes.

To serve, place one generous scoop of ice milk into each of 8 serving dishes, and top with about 2 tablespoons of the gooseberry sauce.

1½ pounds gooseberries, rinsed, stems removed

¾ cup granulated sugar

¼ cup water

1 quart Vanilla Ice Milk (recipe follows) or gourmet ice cream

# Vanilla Ice Milk

*Serves 8*

This is a delicious alternative to the traditional French crème anglaise–based confection. It's much lighter and an uncomplicated recipe for someone who wants to try making ice cream for the first time.

In a 3-quart saucepan, combine the milk and sugar over medium-low heat. Scrape the seeds from the vanilla bean into the mixture, and toss in the scraped bean as well.

Bring the mixture to a rolling boil, stirring occasionally. Lower the heat and simmer for 5 minutes over low heat. Remove the pan from the heat, cover, and set aside to cool to room temperature, about 2½ hours. When the mixture has come to room temperature, transfer the pan to the refrigerator and chill for at least 6 hours or overnight.

Remove the vanilla bean from the pot and pour the milk mixture into an ice-cream maker. Freeze according to the manufacturer's instructions. Freeze in an airtight container until firm. Remove the ice cream from the freezer about 5 minutes before serving to soften.

4 cups milk (any level fat)

⅔ cup granulated sugar

1 vanilla bean, split lengthwise

# Butterfly Luncheon

*Mini Arugula and Scallion Pizzas*

*Grilled Chicken Breasts with Kale Pesto on a
Salad of Garden Vegetables*

*Salted Butter–Caramel Vacherin with
Dark Chocolate Sauce*

*Raspberry, Strawberry, and Rhubarb Jams*

*Chilled White Sancerre*

NE OF THE MOST MAGICAL EVENTS IN THE SUMMER
garden is the arrival of a profusion of butterflies. This is the sign that summer is in full swing.
Fluttering from flower to flower, they are a pleasure to watch. I celebrated nature's show by
hosting an early August luncheon for ten friends in the back of the garden, where we could
view the dance of the butterflies, and also be protected by the afternoon shade.

As most butterflies make their appearance in the late afternoon, when the sun has
begun to set, the tabletop was strewn with colorful artificial ones. The fantasy of the colorful
impostor butterflies wired into local Queen Anne's lace was a lovely substitute until the real
stars appeared. At the start of the day, I bicycled to a roadside bank of Queen Anne's lace
and picked as much as my bike basket could hold. It took several trips to gather enough to
decorate the table.

Given the summer heat, Thomas and I opted for crisp yellow-and-white table runners
in my "Chantal" fabric to complement the green-and-white floral arrangement. White napkins
tied in a simple blue-and-white-striped ribbon were paired with vintage Johnson Brothers
chinoiserie-pattern dinnerware that I purchased at a flea market several years ago.

I love French yogurt. During an extended stay in Paris earlier in the year, I emptied
enough charming old-fashioned jars of yogurt to use as place-card holders for this lunch.
Recycling these jars as charming mementos for guests makes an interesting conversation
starter at the table. The jars, filled with homemade jam and tied with garden twine, were put
at each place setting. I invited my guests to enjoy the jam straight from the jars throughout
the party, slathered on an assortment of local artisanal nut breads.

With the garden producing at full force, there was an abundance of vegetables to
choose from. I opted for delightful mini pizzas topped with arugula and scallions as a
starter, followed by a main course of chicken breasts topped with kale pesto on a bed of
zucchini, tomatoes, green beans, and spinach. A chilled Sancerre paired nicely with this light
fare. Dessert was a rich salted butter–caramel vacherin in a pool of dark chocolate sauce,
which made for a beautiful presentation. The contrast of the sweetness of the caramel with
the savory sea salt is unexpected and wonderful. Since the vacherin was frozen, it was a
refreshing ending to this warm-weather meal.

ABOVE, LEFT: The glorious vivid yellow zucchini bloom can be picked and fried for a tasty side dish, or left to grow until the vegetable matures. ABOVE, RIGHT: Shallots need to stay in direct sunlight for a few days to dry the skins. I spread them out on a large tray. They will keep through the winter when stored in a wicker basket in a cool, dry place. OPPOSITE: I spent the morning of the party biking on country roads to gather enough Queen Anne's lace for the tabletop bouquets.

## TIPS

To prevent cut flowers from wilting, make sure to place them in a vase or container at the last minute.

Early August is an ideal time to start planting lettuce, spinaches, and other autumn garden favorites, such as turnips and baby carrots.

Drying herbs preserves them for cold-weather dishes. One easy technique is to spread the herbs out on a paper towel–lined tray. Leave the tray in a dark, warm, ventilated space for a few days until the herbs dry out.

# Mini Arugula and Scallion Pizzas

*Serves 10*

**M**ini pizzas make a wonderful starter or a light main course, when paired with a salad.

Arrange the racks in the upper and lower thirds of the oven and preheat to 400°F. Line two large baking sheets with parchment paper.

Dust a work surface with flour, then lay the sheets of puff pastry on the surface. Using a 4-inch round pastry cutter, cut the puff pastry into 10 rounds. Prick the pastry rounds with a fork several times, and place them 1½ inches apart on the prepared baking sheets.

Bake for 10 to 15 minutes, until golden brown. Remove the pans from the oven, and set aside.

In a small sauté pan, melt the butter over medium heat. Add the scallions, and cook until tender but not brown, about 5 minutes.

Sprinkle the goat cheese onto the pastry rounds. Divide the scallions into 10 portions and spread a portion on each of the pastry rounds. Return the pastry rounds to the oven for another 10 to 12 minutes, until the cheese is melted. Remove the pastry rounds from the oven and cover each with some of the arugula. Drizzle with the oil and serve immediately.

All-purpose flour

2 packages puff pastry, thawed if frozen

4 tablespoons unsalted butter

2 cups thinly sliced scallions

2 cups crumbled goat cheese

3 cups stemmed arugula, rinsed and dried

6 tablespoons light extra-virgin olive oil

# Grilled Chicken Breasts with Kale Pesto on a Salad of Garden Vegetables

**G**rilling is a simple way to prepare chicken for a crowd. I love the heartiness of this pesto, which also goes well with pasta.

### GRILLED CHICKEN BREASTS

Preheat an outdoor grill or a broiler.

In a large glass bowl, whisk together the oil, salt, and white pepper. Add the chicken to the bowl and turn to coat it in the seasoning mixture.

Grill or broil the chicken for 3 minutes on each side, or until cooked through, then set aside. Cover with plastic wrap until ready to assemble the salad.

### KALE PESTO

Put the kale, walnuts, lemon juice, and garlic in the bowl of a food processor and pulse until coarsely chopped. Add the oil and pulse until combined. Season with the salt and white pepper to taste. Add the cheese and pulse until blended and smooth. Cover with plastic wrap and refrigerate. Remove the pesto from the refrigerator about 20 minutes before you are ready to assemble the salad, so it can come to room temperature.

### SALAD OF GARDEN VEGETABLES

In a large bowl, combine the zucchini, tomatoes, haricots verts, and spinach. Drizzle with the oil and toss to coat.

### TO SERVE

Divide the salad among 10 individual plates and place a chicken breast on top of each serving. Top each portion with 2 tablespoons of the pesto and finish with a sprinkling of fleur de sel. Serve immediately.

**NOTE:** The pesto can be stored in the refrigerator for 1 week in a tightly sealed container.

### GRILLED CHICKEN BREASTS

⅓ cup light extra-virgin olive oil

½ teaspoon fine sea salt

¼ teaspoon freshly ground white pepper

10 boneless, skinless chicken breasts, rinsed and patted dry with paper towels

### KALE PESTO

3 cups stemmed kale leaves, well washed and dried

½ cup walnuts

Juice of ½ lemon

2 garlic cloves, peeled

½ cup light extra-virgin olive oil

¾ teaspoon fine sea salt

Freshly ground white pepper

½ cup freshly grated Parmesan cheese

### SALAD OF GARDEN VEGETABLES

1 large zucchini, trimmed and thinly sliced

1½ cups cherry tomatoes, cut in half

1½ cups trimmed and blanched haricots verts

3 cups baby spinach leaves, trimmed and well washed

2 tablespoons light extra-virgin olive oil

Fleur de sel

# Salted Butter–Caramel Vacherin with Dark Chocolate Sauce

*Serves 8 to 10*

This French dessert takes advance planning but it's well worth the effort. The meringues and vacherin should be made a day ahead. Make the chocolate sauce right before you are ready to serve the vacherin so that the sauce is still warm. If you don't have the time to prep all of the components, it's fine to substitute homemade meringues with good quality store-bought ones.

### MERINGUES

Preheat the oven to 200°F. Line a large baking sheet with parchment paper.

In the bowl of the stand mixer fitted with the whisk attachment, beat the egg whites until soft peaks form. Gradually add the superfine sugar, beating constantly, until the peaks become stiff and glossy.

Transfer the egg-white mixture to a pastry bag fitted with a 1/2-inch plain tip and pipe the meringue mixture into 2-inch discs on the prepared baking sheet, spacing the discs 1 inch apart. Bake the meringues for 2 hours.

Remove the pan from the oven and transfer the meringues to a wire rack to cool before assembling the vacherin.

### SALTED BUTTER–CARAMEL WHIPPED CREAM

Put a large bowl in the refrigerator for 1 hour to chill. Line a 9-by-5-inch loaf pan with parchment paper, leaving a large overhang, and set aside.

In a medium heavy-bottomed nonstick saucepan, warm 2 cups of the cream and set aside. In a second medium heavy-bottomed nonstick saucepan, pour in the sugar, and add the butter. Cook the butter and sugar over medium heat, without stirring, for about 3 minutes until the mixture becomes a pale copper color. Very slowly (be careful of spattering), stir in 1 cup of the warmed cream. Continue to cook for 2 minutes, stirring occasionally. Remove the mixture from the heat and add the remaining 1 cup of warmed cream and the salt. Transfer the caramel sauce to a heatproof bowl and refrigerate, covered with plastic wrap, until chilled.

Put the remaining 1 cup of cream in the large chilled bowl of a stand mixer, fitted with the whisk attachment. In this bowl, whip the cream until stiff peaks form. Fold the whipped cream into the chilled caramel sauce.

### ASSEMBLE

Pour one third of the caramel whipped cream into the prepared loaf pan. Cover the caramel whipped cream with a layer of about eight meringues, arranged closely together. Pour a second third of the caramel whipped cream over the meringues.

### MERINGUES
*(makes about 24)*

4 large egg whites, at room temperature

1 cup superfine sugar

### SALTED BUTTER–CARAMEL WHIPPED CREAM

3 cups heavy cream

3/4 cup granulated sugar

3 tablespoons salted butter

Pinch of sea salt

### DARK CHOCOLATE SAUCE
*(makes 1 1/2 cups)*

4 ounces bittersweet dark chocolate, coarsely chopped

1/4 cup of water

2 tablespoons granulated sugar

1 tablespoon unsalted butter

1 teaspoon instant espresso powder

Add a second layer of 8 meringues, spaced closely together, and top with the last third of the caramel whipped cream.

Cover the filled loaf pan with the overhanging parchment paper. Place the pan in the freezer for at least 6 hours, or until the vacherin is very firm.

### DARK CHOCOLATE SAUCE

Just before you are ready to serve the vacherin, melt the chocolate in the top of a double boiler over very low heat. Meanwhile, in a separate small saucepan, bring the water to a boil. Pour the water into the melted chocolate, mixing well with a wooden spoon. Add the sugar, butter, and espresso powder, and quickly mix with the wooden spoon until smooth. Cook the mixture for another 30 seconds, stirring constantly with the spoon until the sauce is uniform in color and texture.

Remove the double boiler from the heat and pour the sauce into a bowl. Set it aside while you slice the vacherin.

### TO SERVE

Remove the vacherin from the freezer. Carefully take it out of the pan, making sure to peel off and discard all of the parchment paper, and place it on a cutting board. Using a serrated knife, cut the vacherin into slices. Place each slice on a dessert plate and pour the warm chocolate sauce over it (or surround it with a pool of the sauce). Serve immediately.

NOTE: Any leftover meringues can be kept in an airtight container for 1 to 2 weeks.

# Raspberry, Strawberry, and Rhubarb Jams

*Makes 10*
*(4-ounce) jars of jam*

These easy recipes make wonderfully rich jams in no time. Bear in mind that when making jams and preserves, you must use proper canning jars that can be sterilized. (My go-to source for canning instructions is *The Fannie Farmer Cookbook*.) In sterilized jars, these jams will keep for up to 3 months in the refrigerator. If you choose to use containers that cannot be sterilized (like my charming French yogurt jars), make only enough jam for your guests to enjoy at the party or take home, refrigerate, and eat within a day. Serve with artisanal nut breads.

## RASPBERRY JAM

Sterilize the canning jars, lids, and rings (if using), and set aside until ready to use.

In a large nonreactive bowl, mash the raspberries with a wooden spoon. Pour the mashed raspberries into a 5-quart nonreactive saucepan and add the sugar.

Over low heat, slowly bring the mixture to a boil, about 5 to 10 minutes, stirring constantly. Gently skim the foam off the surface as it appears. After the foam has disappeared, boil for 3 additional minutes until the mixture reaches 221°F on an instant-read candy thermometer.

Carefully pour the hot mixture into the prepared jars and let the jam cool completely. Serve the cooled jam immediately, or attach the lids and rings and process the jars in a boiling-water bath.

2 pounds fresh raspberries, picked over and rinsed

2 pounds granulated sugar

## STRAWBERRY JAM

Using the same directions for the Raspberry Jam, substitute 2 pounds of fresh strawberries, hulled and quartered lengthwise, for the raspberries.

## RHUBARB JAM

Sterilize the canning jars, lids, and rings (if using), and set aside until ready to use.

In a large nonreactive bowl, combine all the ingredients in alternating layers. Cover with plastic wrap and refrigerate overnight to macerate.

Pour the rhubarb mixture into a 5-quart nonreactive saucepan. Cook over low heat for 1½ to 2 hours, stirring occasionally, and skimming off any foam that may appear, until the mixture thickens.

Carefully pour the hot mixture into the prepared jars and let the jam cool completely. Serve the cooled jam immediately, or attach the lids and rings and process the jars in a boiling-water bath.

3½ pounds trimmed rhubarb stalks, cut into ½-inch-long pieces

2⅔ pounds granulated sugar

Grated zest of 1 lemon

# Chic
# Summer Soirée

*Tomato Tartare with Parmesan Tuiles*

*Grilled Salmon with Fresh Herbs*

*New Potatoes with Summer Savory*

*Strawberry Charlotte*

*Dry White Chinon*

OPPOSITE: Set for eight, the soirée table sparkles in the glow of candlelight. Reproduction botanical prints are hung on the mirror in floating frames to add depth and color to the bagatelle. OVERLEAF, LEFT: The lush centerpieces were created with an assortment of greens from the garden and accented with stems of wispy white snowdrops and deep purple angelonia. The floral-pattern Herend dinnerware contrasts with the simple glassware. OVERLEAF, RIGHT (clockwise from top left): Decorative details abound—from antique Hitchcock chairs and a crystal salt celler, to a bust of Mercury crowned with ivy and dazzling crystal drops on the chandelier.

T

HE GARDEN IS MY PRIVATE PARADISE—AN OASIS of calm, beauty, and order. All of my guests express these same sentiments when ensconced in the verdant abundance of the garden. When I hosted this late-summer dinner in the bagatelle, I kicked off the evening with a pre-dinner tour of the garden. It was a wonderful way to relax and decompress from the stresses of the day, and it also provided an opportunity to talk about the various things that are growing and to share helpful tips that I have picked up over the years.

Since the bagatelle is without electricity, the dinners are always lit by a large crystal chandelier, which hangs over the table. I love the way the crystals dazzle like prisms, reflecting the candlelight in the full-length mirror that serves as the room's focal point. To add additional light on the table, we generally use some votives. Candlelight is not only romantic; it is also one of the most flattering types of light.

For this particular party, I tented the walls of the bagatelle with yards of my pale green "Dottie" fabric. For a fast makeover, the fabric was made into panels, with a pocket casing at the top that was shirred onto 1-inch lath and nailed to the wall. The tablecloth was made from my "Orangerie" design, inspired by the parquet floors in the Grand Trianon at Versailles. The lattice style of the pattern is ideal for a summer dinner party. Herend dinnerware is one of my weaknesses. I found a beautiful service for sixteen that I use for only special occasions. I mixed the Herend with more casual glasses—green reproduction wine glasses from Williamsburg and clear, vintage Steuben goblets. The clean lines of the glasses contrast well with the sensuous curves of the flowers on the plates.

To take advantage of the bounty of tomatoes, I prepared a delicious tartare using the Teton de Venus tomatoes that I favor. This French heirloom tomato is a wonderful addition to the garden; the fruit is dense and slightly sweet without too many seeds.

Using herbs in cooking is something that I do all the time. By August the herb plants were grown to full size and at their prime for cutting. I combined the fresh flavor of chopped chives and dill to accent the richness of grilled salmon. In my kitchen, summer savory is a constant warm-weather companion to new potatoes. I love the pungent flavor that contrasts with the mildness of the potatoes and the salty butter they are tossed in. The final note of this meal was a cool creamy Strawberry Charlotte. The combination of whipped cream, strawberries, and light, airy ladyfingers was an elegant and blissful end to the meal.

ABOVE: The fuchsia ivy geranium on the
demilune console adds a vibrant note of
color to the *mise-en-scène*. RIGHT: Lanterns
along the allée light the way through the
lush garden to dinner in the bagatelle.

# Tomato Tartare with Parmesan Tuiles

Using a variety of multicolored heirloom tomatoes makes this starter as visually appealing as it is tasty for this summer dish.

### TOMATO TARTARE

Place a plastic colander over a large bowl and set aside. Fill a large bowl with ice water and set next to the stovetop.

Bring a large pot of water to a boil over medium-high heat. Blanch the tomatoes in the boiling water for 1 minute, remove them from the pot, and immediately submerge them in the ice water bath to stop their cooking. Peel the tomatoes (the skins should slip right off), then remove and discard their seeds and dice them into 1/2-inch pieces. Place the diced tomatoes in the colander and let drain for 30 minutes, tossing a few times.

When the tomatoes have drained, transfer them to a large bowl. Add the parsley, cilantro, shallot, garlic, salt, and pepper. Taste the salad, and adjust the seasonings as necessary.

Line eight 3/4-cup ramekins with plastic wrap, leaving a 2-inch overhang. Fill each ramekin with 1/2 cup of the tomato mixture and press down to mold.

Invert each tartare onto an individual serving plate, and remove the plastic wrap. Garnish with a Parmesan Tuile just before serving. The tartare can be made 1 hour ahead and set aside at room temperature.

### PARMESAN TUILES

Preheat the oven to 350°F.

Line two baking sheets with parchment paper. Place a 3-inch round cookie cutter on the parchment and drop 3 tablespoons of the cheese inside the cookie cutter. With an offset spatula, spread the cheese evenly and then lift the cookie cutter and move it to a clean spot on the parchment, 2 inches from the first circle. Repeat with the rest of the Parmesan, leaving 2 inches between each circle of cheese, 6 per baking sheet.

Bake the cheese circles for 10 to 12 minutes, until they are completely melted and have turned golden brown. Remove the baking sheet from the oven and, with a metal spatula, quickly transfer the tuiles to a tuile mold to shape, or drape over a rolling pin. Let cool. These can be made 30 minutes ahead, but if it is a humid day, serve them immediately, before the moisture makes them lose their crispness.

### TOMATO TARTARE

4 medium red tomatoes (about 1 pound), such as Teton de Venus

4 medium yellow or green heirloom tomatoes (about 1 pound), such as Green Zebra

2 tablespoons finely chopped fresh flat-leaf parsley

1 tablespoon finely chopped fresh cilantro

1 shallot, finely minced

1 garlic clove, finely minced

3/4 teaspoon fine sea salt

Coarsely ground black pepper

### PARMESAN TUILES
*(Makes 12 tuiles)*

2 1/4 cups freshly grated Parmesan cheese

# Grilled Salmon with Fresh Herbs

*Serves 8*

This is one of my favorite ways to make salmon; I love the freshness of the herbs against the richness of the fish. It does, however, require some advance planning. Make sure you allot at least 3 hours for the fish to marinate.

In a shallow dish, make the marinade: Mix together the oil and Worcestershire sauce. Season the salmon fillets with the salt and pepper, dip them in the marinade to coat, then place them in a glass baking dish and pour any remaining marinade over top. Cover with plastic wrap and refrigerate for 3 to 6 hours.

Preheat the grill or broiler. Grill or broil the salmon for 4 minutes per side, or until cooked through. Serve immediately, topped with the dill and chives.

⅓ cup extra-virgin olive oil

1 teaspoon Worcestershire sauce

8 (8-ounce) portions Atlantic salmon fillet

½ teaspoon fine sea salt

1 teaspoon coarsely ground black pepper

¼ cup finely chopped fresh dill

¼ cup finely chopped fresh chives

# New Potatoes with Summer Savory

*Serves 8*

Freshly harvested new potatoes tossed with butter and summer savory is just the thing for any summer meal. They go with just about anything, and leftovers can be chopped and sautéed the next morning for breakfast alongside scrambled eggs.

Bring a large pot of water to a boil over medium-high heat. Add the potatoes to the boiling water and cook for 10 to 12 minutes, or until fork tender. While the potatoes are cooking, melt the butter in a small saucepan over very low heat.

Drain the potatoes in a colander, then return them to the hot empty pot, and gently toss to evaporate excess moisture.

Pour the butter over the potatoes, add the salt and summer savory, and toss to combine. Serve hot.

30 to 36 heirloom new potatoes of similar size, scrubbed

1 cup (2 sticks) unsalted butter

1 tablespoon coarse sea salt

6 tablespoons fresh summer savory leaves, chopped

# Strawberry Charlotte

A delicate and light charlotte made with bright summer strawberries and cream is a delightful end to a meal. Since it needs at least 6 hours to chill and set, it's also a great make-ahead dessert that you can simply get from the refrigerator after dinner is done.

Set aside 8 whole strawberries to use as a garnish. In a blender, pulse the remaining strawberries with the superfine sugar, leaving some large pieces to add texture to the mousse.

In a small pan over medium heat, bring $1/2$ cup of the strawberry puree to a boil. Remove the pan from the heat and, using a wooden spoon or silicone spatula, stir in the gelatin until the mixture is smooth and thoroughly combined. Add the remaining puree to the pan, stirring constantly. Measure out $1/4$ cup of the puree mixture, and pour it into a small bowl. Remove the pan from the heat, and set aside to cool.

In the bowl of a stand mixer fitted with the whisk attachment, beat the cream at medium-low speed until soft peaks form, then gradually increase the speed until the peaks are stiff and glossy. Using a silicone spatula, gently fold in the strawberry-gelatin mixture.

Line the bottom of a nonstick charlotte mold or 8-inch springform pan with parchment paper. One by one, dip the ladyfingers quickly into the reserved strawberry puree and arrange them in a single layer on a plate. Brush the bottom of the pan with the remaining puree. Line the sides of the pan with the moistened ladyfingers, sugar side out. Pour in the mousse and arrange the remaining ladyfingers on top.

Cover the mold with plastic wrap and refrigerate for at least 6 hours or until well set.

When you are ready to serve, carefully invert the charlotte onto a serving plate and garnish with the remaining whole strawberries.

1¼ pounds of strawberries, washed and hulled

⅔ cups super fine sugar

1 (¼-ounce) package of Knox unflavored gelatin

2 cups heavy cream

1 package (about 20) good-quality ladyfingers

# Casual Fall Buffet

Rosemary Fougasse

*Oeufs en Cocotte
with Mixed Green Salad*

*Raspberry Tart*

*Red Burgundy*

**T**HE EARLY EVENING HOURS ARE A WONDERFUL TIME to be in the garden, especially in September, when the air is cooler and the sun casts long shafts of light over the season's many blooms. It's the time of year when casual drinks often turn into spur-of-the-moment dinner parties, with the help of a few simple recipes and what is on hand in the garden.

The gravel-paved seating area is where we casually entertain, surrounded by lush hydrangeas, an assortment of potted plants, roses climbing up the wall, and, of course, loads of nicotiana that perfumes the air with its luscious scent. We were lucky that night because the urns on the demilune were filled with plumbago in full bloom. The rich blue of the plumbago is incomparable and always a pleasure to behold.

For this particular impromptu buffet-style dinner, I combined two of my fabrics, using laminated "Combray Duo" for the trays and "Venice Scarlet" for the napkins. For dinnerware, I selected everyday vintage Wood & Sons cream plates, with rope-edge details, as well as retro walnut-handled flatware. The flowers were simple, single stems in clear glass containers, and lots of votives completed the setting.

For the meal, I used the abundant leeks, salad greens, and raspberries in the garden. I purchased fresh organic local eggs for the main course. The salad came together with a few snips from the rows of La Grosse Blonde Paresseuse and Craquerelle du Midi lettuces, and for extra flavor, I added a bit of dill and tossed the salad with a simple vinaigrette. I love the combination of eggs and leeks. For the entrée, I served a delicious, easy-to-make Oeufs en Cocotte with braised leeks. I first learned about this amazingly versatile dish when I was a culinary student in Paris, and since then, it has been my go-to recipe for a quick and nutritious meal. The leeks I used are my favorite variety, Bleu de Solaise. I pick them when they are young and more tender than some of the larger ones commonly found in the market; that way they require only a quick sauté in some butter.

Since this buffet was held in early September, the raspberries were producing again after their annual summer hiatus, which lasts from the end of July to late August. What could be easier than a raspberry tart? Although I am not a fan of frozen pie crusts, I always have frozen puff-pastry sheets on hand to make tart shells. I like the lighter texture, and they help make last-minute dinners possible.

OPPOSITE: Tray dinners are a wonderful way to entertain. The pressure of setting the table is alleviated for the host. Napkins folded to hold flatware make them easy to arrange on the buffet table. A display of hydrangeas graces the tablescape. OVERLEAF, LEFT: This impromptu dinner came together easily due to a well-stocked garden and a few simple recipes. OVERLEAF, RIGHT (clockwise from top left): A flat platter makes cutting a tart easy. A striking centerpiece for the cocktail table was created by placing single stems of marigolds and zinnias in five small glass vases set in a row. Lids keep the Oeufs en Cocotte warm. Red goblets complement the napkins and trays.

The seating area is a verdant
oasis of late-summer calm.
At this point in the season,
the plants are at their peak.
The glorious plumbagos
are blooming freely, the
hydrangeas have matured,
and the ivy covering the fence
has totally grown in.

ABOVE, LEFT: Nicotiana not only has a stunning flower, it also has a sensual fragrance. ABOVE, RIGHT: Bleu de Solaise is a French heirloom leek known for its blue-green foliage. La Grosse Blonde Paresseuse, a flavorful and tender French heirloom lettuce, makes wonderful salads. OPPOSITE: The iron urns on the demilune filled with plumbago. Paired with flickering white candles in pewter candlesticks and blue-and-white pieces, the rich blue flowering bush pops.

## TIPS

- To help reduce wax dripping when burning candles, I always freeze them for a couple of hours before using.

- Now is the time to create next year's beautiful lawn. Reseeding and fertilizing in the fall will ensure green grass the following summer.

- Take copious notes and make a detailed plan for next year's garden. Keep planting times in mind and figure out which plants will survive the winter and come back the following spring.

# Rosemary Fougasse

Although this recipe is inspired by the traditional French bread, it uses baking powder instead of yeast. The rosemary adds a robust flavor that complements the olives beautifully.

Preheat the oven to 375°F. Line a baking sheet with parchment paper, and set aside.

In a large bowl, with a wooden spoon, combine the flour, baking powder, 2 tablespoons oil, olives, salt, and rosemary. Mix well.

Add the water a little at a time, mixing after each addition, until the dough is supple and not sticky.

Cut the dough into four equal pieces. Turn the dough out onto a floured work surface and quickly knead it into four individual ovals. Place the ovals on the prepared baking sheet. With a small sharp knife, make 3 diagonal slits in the top of each oval.

Brush each loaf with a little oil and bake for 20 minutes, or until golden brown. Serve warm.

2 cups all-purpose flour

1 ½ teaspoons baking powder

2 tablespoons olive oil, plus more for brushing

¼ cup pitted black olives, chopped

½ teaspoon salt

2 tablespoons chopped fresh rosemary

⅔ cup water

# Oeufs en Cocotte

*Serves 4*

Eggs, cream, leeks, and Gruyère, slowly baked—what could be better for a satisfying entrée? Serve with a mixed green salad for a complete meal. *(See page 121)*

Preheat the oven to 325°F. Butter four 6-inch gratin dishes. Place the dishes in a large baking dish.

In a small sauté pan, melt 2 tablespoons of butter over medium-low heat. Add the leeks and cook for 5 minutes, or until they are translucent, stirring occasionally. Set aside.

Reserve 2 ounces of the cheese for topping. Sprinkle the remaining 6 ounces of cheese evenly in the dishes. Evenly divide the leeks in the dishes and place on top of the cheese. Place a pat of butter (about 1 tablespoon) on top of the leeks in each dish. Break 2 eggs into each dish. Pour 2 tablespoons of cream on top of the eggs and top with the reserved cheese. Sprinkle lightly with salt and pepper.

Fill the large baking pan with enough hot water to reach halfway up the sides of the dishes, being careful not to splash any water into the dishes.

Bake the eggs for 15 minutes, or until the whites have set but the yolks are still soft. Remove them from the oven and let them cool slightly. Garnish with the chopped parsley and serve warm.

6 tablespoons unsalted butter, plus more for the baking dishes

6 medium leeks, white parts only coarsely chopped into ½-inches pieces, trimmed and cleaned thoroughly

8 ounces Gruyère or Swiss chees, coarsely grated

8 large eggs

8 tablespoons heavy cream

Fine sea salt

Freshly ground black pepper

2 tablespoons roughly chopped fresh Italian flat-leaf parsley

Mixed Green Salad and Vinaigrette (see page 25 for recipe, but add a few sprigs dill, finely chopped.)

# Raspberry Tart

*Serves 6*

This tart comes together in a jiffy, due in part to the use of pre-made puff pastry. The tapioca in the bottom is flavorless, but it absorbs the juice from the berries, which keeps the tart from being too runny. *(See page 121.)*

Preheat the oven to 400°F.

Line a 10-inch removable-bottom tart pan with the puff pastry. Blind-bake the pastry in the oven for 10 minutes, or until it turns a light golden brown. Keep the oven on. Remove the tart shell from the oven, and set it aside to cool.

Once the tart shell has cooled, sprinkle the tapioca and 1 tablespoon of the sugar into the shell. Neatly arrange the raspberries on top, and sprinkle with the remaining 2 tablespoons of sugar.

Bake the tart for 25 minutes, or until the berries are soft but still firm. Remove the tart from the oven and let it cool on a rack for 10 minutes before serving.

1 sheet puff pastry, thawed if frozen

1 tablespoon instant tapioca

3 tablespoons granulated sugar

2 cups fresh raspberries, rinsed and patted dry

# Early Autumn Dinner

Tomato Soup

◆

Roasted Rosemary Chicken au Jus

◆

Puree of Turnips, Carrots, and Potatoes

◆

Pumpkin Cake Roll

◆

Côte de Beaune Rouge

OPPOSITE: This autumn table is a work of art. The vegetable topiaries are worth the effort, creating a one-of-a-kind decoration for a special evening. OVERLEAF, LEFT: The ambers, browns, and tans of the glasses, fabric, flatware, and service plates made the perfect background for the bright vegetables. OVERLEAF, RIGHT (clockwise from top left): Gold-washed votives cast a glow on the table. I love using colored glasses for reflective warmth. They add personality to a table setting. A lovely ceramic artichoke was found in a Venetian shop. The haricots verts topiary required stringing beans together with thread and draping them over a moss-covered Styrofoam cone.

I CONSIDER THE MOST BEAUTIFUL MONTH IN THE garden to be September. The plants are still producing their treasures and thriving, in spite of the shortened days. The heat of the summer has long abated, and the evenings have a refreshing crispness. Perhaps the biggest treat of all is a lull in the heavy gardening work, and knowing there is time to really relax before the autumn cleanup starts in November. It is as if the plants know that this is their last hurrah.

To take advantage of this splendid period and to unabashedly show off the garden one last time, I hosted a seated dinner for eight. I created a harvest dinner mood for the table by echoing the vegetables that were in the garden in either ceramic or topiary forms. It was a terrific opportunity to show off my extensive collection of ceramic vegetables, which I have amassed over the years from my travels. I have a wonderful assortment of exquisite vegetables from a small shop in Venice, and realistic mushrooms I bought from a dealer in Paris, to name a few. I am a firm believer that any collection accumulated over time has much more charm than one acquired in a single shopping spree.

To make sure that the table was a standout, in lieu of flowers, I decided to craft vegetable topiaries. I was inspired by the Italian Capodimonte pieces I had seen in a chateau during a visit to France. My topiaries were not made of the traditional ceramic pieces; instead I hot-glued real vegetables in place and sculpted them to create one-of-a-kind objects.

For the tablecloth, I chose one of my more formal fabrics, "Beekman," in a soft neutral camel color, and for each setting, I layered Mottahedeh leaf salad plates on milky brown service plates. Amber glasses and tortoise flatware completed the color scheme.

The menu reflects the abundance of the garden. We started the meal with a tomato soup made from the end-of-season tomatoes and onions from the garden. I find chicken to be one of the most versatile meats for entertaining. For the main course, I roasted a whole chicken with butter and rosemary, and served it with a puree of vegetables and potatoes. The meal ended with an autumnal pumpkin cake roll.

## TIPS

❀ When creating topiaries like the ones featured for this dinner, using fresh, blemish-free vegetables is critical.

❀ As the nights get cooler and the first frost approaches, I keep protective covers for the more delicate plants at the ready. Protecting the plants can help extend the growing seasons of certain varieties, such as tomatoes, citrus, plumbago, and geraniums.

❀ Any green tomatoes lingering in the garden can be ripened on a sunny windowsill or made into delicious jam.

RIGHT: These topiaries are a symphony of autumn abundance. OVERLEAF, LEFT (clockwise from top left): Purple-top turnips are hardy root vegetables. The blue-green leaves of Brussels sprouts. Brussels sprouts have great flavor when picked after the first frost. Milkmaid nasturtiums make a great addition to salad. The peppery-flavored leaves are also edible. A basket holds lettuces to be transplanted in the winter garden. OVERLEAF, RIGHT: A variety of cold-tolerant lettuces and spinach. St. Fiacre, the patron saint of gardens, stands guard among the plants.

AN INVITATION TO THE GARDEN

# Tomato Soup

This is a wonderful dairy-free soup that is easy to make, but be warned: The cayenne pepper gives it a spicy kick. For a milder version, reduce the cayenne to ¼ teaspoon. It is great hot or chilled and freezes really well.

Heat the oil in a large 5-quart pot over medium heat, add the onion and garlic, and cook until the onion is translucent, about 5 minutes. Do not let the onion brown. Add the fresh tomatoes, zucchini, sun-dried tomatoes, cayenne, sugar, salt, and pepper to taste and simmer for 25 minutes. Add the stock, and cook for an additional 15 minutes.

 Remove the pot from the heat and puree the soup using an immersion blender, or pour into a blender, in batches if necessary, let cool for a few minutes, and blend until smooth. Taste and add more salt and pepper, as needed. Stir in the parsley, cover, and refrigerate for at least 6 hours before serving. This soup can be frozen for up to 3 months.

2 tablespoons extra-virgin olive oil

1 large yellow onion, chopped

6 garlic cloves, peeled and chopped

3 pounds red tomatoes, quartered

3 medium zucchini, peeled and chopped

¼ cup sun-dried tomatoes

½ teaspoon cayenne pepper

½ teaspoon granulated sugar

½ teaspoon coarse sea salt, or more if needed

Freshly ground black pepper

2 cups vegetable stock

3 tablespoons finely chopped fresh Italian flat-leaf parsley

# Puree of Turnips, Carrots, and Potatoes

*Serves 8*

I love this mix of autumn vegetables. The carrots add a note of sweetness and a bit of perk to the puree's otherwise creamy-white color.

Fill a large pot with cold water and add the turnips, carrots, potatoes, and salt. Bring to a boil over medium heat and cook the vegetables for 20 to 30 minutes, until they are fork tender.

 Drain the vegetables in a large colander, and return them to the hot pot to evaporate any excess moisture. Add the butter to the vegetables and, using a hand mixer or immersion blender, cream them together on high speed. Add the warmed cream and continue mixing until the puree is smooth. Taste and season with salt and pepper. Serve immediately.

2 pounds turnips, peeled and quartered

1 pound carrots, peeled and roughly chopped

1 pound potatoes, peeled and quartered

½ teaspoon fine sea salt, plus more for finishing

½ cup (1 stick) unsalted butter, at room temperature

¼ cup heavy cream, warmed slightly

Freshly ground black pepper

# Roasted Rosemary Chicken au Jus

Roasted chicken is one of my favorite comfort foods. I find that searing the chicken at a high temperature helps to keep the bird moist and tender.

Preheat the oven to 450°F.

Season the chicken's cavity with salt and pepper, and stuff it with 4 tablespoons of the butter and half of the rosemary.

Loosen the skin of the chicken with your fingers, being careful not to tear it. Slip 2 tablespoons of the remaining butter and a few sprigs of the remaining rosemary under the skin. Using your fingers, rub the remaining 2 tablespoons of butter all over the outside of the chicken, and season generously with salt and pepper.

Transfer the chicken to a flameproof 9-by-13-inch baking pan and roast for 20 minutes, or until the skin begins to brown, then lower the oven temperature to 350°F and continue cooking for 45 minutes more, basting from time to time with the pan drippings. The chicken should be medium-brown in color, and the juices should run clear when the leg is pierced. To double-check for doneness, insert a meat thermometer into the thickest part of a leg. The temperature will read 165°F when fully cooked.

Remove the pan from the oven and lift the chicken onto a carving board. Let it rest for 10 minutes while you make the sauce.

Place the pan with the juices on the stove over medium heat. Add the wine and let the liquid simmer for 8 to 10 minutes, or until it has reduced to about ⅔ cup.

Carve the chicken, and serve it drizzled with the sauce.

1 whole (3-pound) chicken, rinsed and patted dry

Fine sea salt and freshly ground black pepper

8 tablespoons (1 stick) unsalted butter, at room temperature

1 bunch fresh rosemary

½ cup dry white wine

# Pumpkin Cake Roll

I was taught how to make this cake back home by my dear neighbor Karen Stransky. She was like a surrogate mother to me after my own mother died, and she taught me all the fundamentals that I know about cooking. Without her guidance, I would not have the interest or skills in cooking that I do.

Position a rack in the center of the oven and preheat to 375°F.

### CAKE

Line a jelly-roll pan with parchment paper; spray the paper with nonstick cooking spray and dust with flour, shaking off any excess.

In the bowl of a stand mixer fitted with the paddle attachment, beat the eggs until they turn pale yellow. Gradually add the sugar, then the pumpkin and lemon juice, and mix until smooth and uniform in color.

Place a sheet of parchment paper on your work surface. Using a fine-mesh sieve, sift the flour, baking powder, cinnamon, ginger, nutmeg, and salt onto the parchment. Add the sifted dry ingredients to the pumpkin mixture and mix well with a wooden spoon.

Pour the batter into the prepared pan and bake for 15 minutes, or until the cake springs back to the touch.

Lay a clean dish towel on a work surface and dust it with confectioners' sugar. Carefully invert the hot cake onto the towel and roll it up in the towel, starting from one of the narrow ends. Let the cake cool while you prepare the frosting.

### FILLING AND FROSTING

In a stand mixer fitted with the paddle attachment, beat the confectioners' sugar, cream cheese, butter, and vanilla until smooth and creamy.

### ASSEMBLE

Unroll the cooled cake and remove the towel. Spread half of the frosting evenly on the cake, then sprinkle half of the pecans over the top. Reroll the cake starting at a narrow end. Frost the sides and top of the rolled cake with the remaining frosting and sprinkle with the remaining pecans. Cover the cake loosely with foil and refrigerate for at least 3 hours before serving.

## CAKE

3 large eggs

1 cup granulated sugar

¾ cup pure pumpkin puree, canned or fresh (drained well if it is fresh puree)

1 teaspoon freshly squeezed lemon juice

¾ cup all-purpose flour

1 teaspoon baking powder

2 teaspoons ground cinnamon

½ teaspoon ground ginger

½ teaspoon freshly grated nutmeg

½ teaspoon salt

Confectioners' sugar

## FILLING AND FROSTING

2 cups confectioners' sugar

2 (8-ounce) packages cream cheese, at room temperature

½ cup (1 stick) unsalted butter, at room temperature

1½ teaspoons vanilla extract

2 cups chopped pecans

# Harvest Lunch

*Savory Cake of Ham, Goat Cheese, and Figs*

*Fall Salad with Mustard Vinaigrette*

*Poulet Pot-au-Feu*

*Chocolate Fondue with Miniature Pastry Puffs*

*Pinot Noir and Pinot Blanc*

*Peppermint Tea*

A**S THE AUTUMN DAYS GREW SHORTER** and chillier, the warmth of a sudden blast of Indian summer was much appreciated in early November, making the obligatory end-of-season cleanup and leaf-raking much more enjoyable.

After several frosts, the bright array of summer vegetables and flowers had dimmed, and the colors were replaced by the more subtle tones of autumn kale, blue pansies, leeks, Brussels sprouts, and various root vegetables and winter lettuces. Inspired by the unseasonably warm weather, I decided to plan a final alfresco meal in the garden before the end of the year. A relaxed lunch for eight came together quickly.

To keep things simple, I brought the table that is used in the bagatelle outside. It was given a quick makeover by stapling natural linen to the top and hot gluing some smart wood beaded trim to its edge. The chairs were inexpensive Ikea finds, dressed up in slipcovers in various patterns from my collection. To unite this colorful display, I accented the slipcovers with dark red grosgrain-ribbon trim.

The meal began with a Savory Cake of Ham, Goat Cheese, and Figs, along with a simple salad of fall lettuces tossed in a mustard vinaigrette. The main course was one of my favorite cold-weather dishes, a simple Poulet Pot-au-Feu. Using chicken instead of beef makes this a much lighter alternative to the traditional French beef-based pot-au-feu. I prepared this hearty dish with carrots, turnips, and leeks from the garden. Dessert was a decadent chocolate fondue. There's something magical about serving fondue; it brings back fond childhood memories. We dipped mini pastry puffs into the dark chocolate for a messy ending to a scrumptious meal.

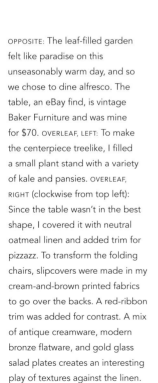

OPPOSITE: The leaf-filled garden felt like paradise on this unseasonably warm day, and so we chose to dine alfresco. The table, an eBay find, is vintage Baker Furniture and was mine for $70. OVERLEAF, LEFT: To make the centerpiece treelike, I filled a small plant stand with a variety of kale and pansies. OVERLEAF, RIGHT (clockwise from top left): Since the table wasn't in the best shape, I covered it with neutral oatmeal linen and added trim for pizzazz. To transform the folding chairs, slipcovers were made in my cream-and-brown printed fabrics to go over the backs. A red-ribbon trim was added for contrast. A mix of antique creamware, modern bronze flatware, and gold glass salad plates creates an interesting play of textures against the linen.

ABOVE, LEFT: I use glass cloches to protect tender plants from the frost. ABOVE, RIGHT: Colorful kale makes a spectacular centerpiece. RIGHT: For fall cleanup, I rake leaves into vintage peach baskets for compost to be used the following summer.

## TIPS

❧ Keep a variety of cloches in different sizes to protect plants from frost in the fall and to help speed germination in the spring.

❧ One of the easiest ways to make compost each fall is to use simple black garbage bags. I fill them with leaves, tie them loosely, and let them sit until late summer. By then, Mother Nature has worked her magic and I have a wonderful source of rich and fertile soil for spring planting.

❧ Many root vegetables will continue growing in the garden throughout the winter. To make sure they are retrievable in the coldest months, cover them with a 6-inch layer of straw to insulate the ground and make it possible to dig them out.

# Savory Cake of Ham, Goat Cheese, and Figs

*Serves 8*

This flavorful cake can be made a day ahead, wrapped in plastic wrap, and refrigerated until ready to use. Warming it just before serving will enhance the flavors.

Preheat the oven to 350°F. Butter and flour a 9-by-5-inch loaf pan and set aside.

In a large bowl, whisk together the flour, baking powder, and salt. Using a wooden spoon or silicone spatula, gently mix in the eggs, one at a time. Mix well until the dough is firm. Slowly add the milk and oil, and mix until thoroughly combined. Fold in the goat cheese, ham, and figs until they are thoroughly incorporated, being careful not to blend the cheese.

Pour the mixture into the prepared pan, and bake for 45 to 55 minutes, or until a toothpick inserted in the center comes out clean. Remove the pan from the oven and place it on a wire rack to cool for 5 minutes. Remove the cake from the pan and, using a serrated knife, cut it into ¾-inch slices. Serve the cake while still warm, but not hot.

Unsalted butter for the pan

1⅔ cups all-purpose flour

2 teaspoons baking powder

½ teaspoon fine sea salt

3 large eggs

½ cup whole milk

½ cup vegetable oil

8 ounces goat cheese, crumbled

4 ounces cooked ham steak, diced into ½-inch cubes (about 1 cup)

½ cup coarsely chopped fresh figs

# Fall Salad with Mustard Vinaigrette

*Serves 8*

This mustard-based vinaigrette is thick and rather creamy. Its robust flavor makes it a perfect match for the strong flavors of autumn lettuces such as radicchio and escarole.

Put the mustard in a small glass bowl and, whisking constantly with a fork or small whisk, add the oil a drop at a time, incorporating until blended. After you have added about 2 tablespoons of the oil, pour the remaining 4 tablespoons into the bowl in a thin stream, whisking constantly. This process should take about 7 minutes, and the mixture should be very smooth and uniform in color.

Add the vinegar, then the salt and pepper to taste, and whisk the mixture to combine. The vinaigrette should be thick and creamy. Just before serving, stir in the boiling water.

Put the salad greens in a large serving bowl and toss them with the vinaigrette. Serve immediately.

1½ tablespoons Dijon mustard

6 tablespoons walnut oil

2 teaspoons red wine vinegar

Fine sea salt

Freshly ground black pepper

1 tablespoon boiling water

8 ounces mixed autumn salad greens, washed and dried

# Poulet Pot-au-Feu

*Serves 8*

This is my take on a classic French dish, made with chicken instead of the usual beef. Serve it with an earthy country bread, cornichons, mustard, and coarse salt.

Put the chicken in a very large pot and cover it with water. Bring the water to a boil over medium-high heat and cook for 8 to 10 minutes.

Remove the chicken from the pot and discard the cooking liquid. Wipe out the pot, and return the chicken to it. Cover the chicken again with fresh water and add the wine, carrots, turnips, leeks, and onion. Cover the pot and bring to a boil over medium-high heat. As soon as the liquid comes to a rolling boil, reduce the heat to low, add the bouquet garni, and season to taste with salt and pepper. Cover the pot and simmer over low heat for 1½ hours, or until the chicken starts to fall off the bone.

Remove the chicken and vegetables from the stock, keeping the pot over low heat, and place the chicken, garnished with two to three parsley sprigs, and vegetables on a serving platter. Cover the platter with foil to keep everything warm until ready to serve.

Increase the heat to medium-high and cook the stock until it has reduced by one-quarter, about 20 minutes. Serve the stock immediately in individual bowls and let your guests help themselves to the chicken and vegetables at the table. (Alternatively, you can serve the stock as a light first course to precede the chicken and vegetables.)

1 whole (3- to 4-pound) stewing hen

½ bottle dry white wine

4 medium carrots, peeled and quartered

2 large turnips, peeled and quartered

4 large leeks, green parts discarded, white parts cut in half lengthwise

1 onion studded with 6 whole cloves

1 bouquet garni (see page 52)

Fine sea salt and freshly ground black pepper

20 small sprigs fresh flat-leaf Italian parsley, for garnish

## PEPPERMINT TEA

This mint tea goes well with chocolate. It can be made ahead of time and kept in a thermos until ready to use.

8 mint sprigs, rinsed
8 cups boiling water
Sugar or honey, for serving

Put the mint sprigs in a teapot and pour the boiling water over them. Let the tea steep for 6 to 8 minutes, then remove the mint and serve the tea in teacups with sugar or honey. *Serves 8*

# Chocolate Fondue with Miniature Pastry Puffs

*Serves 8*

Chocolate fondue is a fun and festive way to end a meal. The miniature cream puffs can be made several hours before serving and kept at room temperature in an airtight container until ready to use.

### PASTRY PUFFS

Preheat the oven to 400°F. Set aside an ungreased baking sheet.

In a 3-quart saucepan, combine the water, butter, salt, and sugar over medium heat. Stir the mixture with a wooden spoon until the butter has melted, then remove the pan from the heat and add the flour all at once. Return the pan to the stove over a low heat, and stir until the dough forms a ball, 2 to 3 minutes.

Remove the pan from the heat, and transfer the dough to a large glass mixing bowl. Let it rest for about 5 minutes. Add the eggs, one at a time, completely incorporating each one before adding the next. Repeat until all of the eggs have been added and the dough is smooth.

Drop rounded teaspoons of the dough onto an ungreased baking sheet, leaving about 2 inches between the mounds. Bake for about 20 minutes, or until the dough puffs up and turns golden brown, and a toothpick inserted into the center of a puff comes out clean.

Remove the baking sheet from the oven, and transfer the puffs to a wire rack to cool completely before serving.

### FONDUE

In the top of a double boiler, melt the chocolate over low heat, stirring constantly with a wooden spoon.

Remove the pan from the heat, and pour the chocolate mixture into a fondue pot. Heat the fondue pot according to the manufacturer's directions and keep it warm until ready to serve.

### TO SERVE

Stick skewers or fondue forks into the puffs and place them on a large platter alongside the fondue pot, so that your guests can dip the puffs into the fondue.

### PASTRY PUFFS
*(Makes 28 to 32)*

1 cup water

5 tablespoons unsalted butter, cut into pieces

½ teaspoon salt

½ teaspoon granulated sugar

1 cup all-purpose flour

4 large eggs, at room temperature

### FONDUE

1½ pounds 60% dark chocolate, coarsely chopped

# Early Winter Dinner

Brussels Sprouts with Bacon

Blanquette de Veau

Tarte Tatin

Red Burgundy

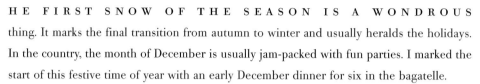

**T**HE FIRST SNOW OF THE SEASON IS A WONDROUS thing. It marks the final transition from autumn to winter and usually heralds the holidays. In the country, the month of December is usually jam-packed with fun parties. I marked the start of this festive time of year with an early December dinner for six in the bagatelle.

The decor was inspired by my passion for pattern. I have always thought there is something magical about using a single print throughout a room. For this party, I took that concept to the extreme and covered almost everything—the walls, table, chairs, and even the dinnerware—in my "Thomas" design. The walls were tightly upholstered, which created a more tailored look, which I felt this type of decor required. The chairs were draped in one length of fabric that fastened at the sides. The "Thomas" dinnerware was hand-painted by Marie Daâge and completed the pattern-on-pattern layering.

Since the winter season is not known for its garden blooms, the centerpiece arrangements were made from antique German metal leaves and flowers that I found at the Brimfield flea market. I arranged them in various terra-cotta pots and little alabaster vases. The patina of the flowers and the texture of the pots complemented the worn finish of the vintage Italian silver-plated candelabras, which lit the space that evening.

For glassware, I used one of my favorites, white French opaline by Portieux Vallerysthal. My collection dates from the 1960s and has a clean modern look, and it worked beautifully with the mellow luster of my pewter flatware.

There is nothing like freshly picked Brussels sprouts to start off a cold-weather meal. I parboiled the Brussels sprouts to help speed the cooking time and married them with white wine, pork shoulder bacon, and onions.

The main course was one of my favorite dishes, Blanquette de Veau, a French ragout of veal in a thickened white sauce. It is really not a complex dish to make, but the more time it has to cook, the more tender and magical the result. And for dessert, who could resist a classic Tarte Tatin, made with apples from local orchards and topped with fluffy crème fraîche?

Inspired by the snowy setting of *Dr. Zhivago*, I printed my "Thomas" fabric in gray for this romantic evening. Surfaces throughout the room were covered in it, and chairs were transformed by draping a piece of the fabric secured with Velcro. Since the winter is a barren period for the garden, centerpieces made of antique tole leaves and flowers were used. OVERLEAF, LEFT: The hand-painted "Thomas" plates mimic my "Thomas" fabric. OVERLEAF, RIGHT (clockwise from top left): The salt cellar, decorated in silver leaf, and its mother-of-pearl spoon add a winter sparkle. Blanquette de Veau is a satisfying dish for a cold night. This set of rare vintage French opaline glasses is used for special occasions. Contemporary napkin rings complement the decor.

## TIPS

🌼 Early winter is a great time to clean, sharpen, and wax the garden tools so they will be ready to go back to work in a few months' time.

🌼 Be sure to empty the water from watering cans, especially vintage galvanized ones, and sprayers that are exposed to the cold before they freeze and crack.

🌼 This is the moment to go through the garden and label the perennials so you'll know where they'll be blooming next spring.

🌼 Northern Spy apples are excellent for baking since they always hold their shape when cooked.

LEFT, TOP AND BOTTOM, AND OPPOSITE: A gentle snow falls on the garden, covering a lantern and hydrangea. The Brussels sprouts will remain in the garden until they are needed in the kitchen.

# Brussels Sprouts with Bacon

Finishing this dish under the broiler adds a wonderful crispness to all of the ingredients.

Preheat the broiler.

Bring a large pot of water to a boil over high heat. Add the Brussels sprouts and cook for 5 minutes in the boiling water, then immediately remove them with a slotted spoon and transfer them to a colander to drain.

In a large cast-iron skillet, sauté the bacon pieces over medium-high heat until just lightly browned, about 4 minutes. Add the onion and continue cooking until they are softened and lightly browned, about 5 minutes.

Add the Brussels sprouts and wine to the skillet and cook for about 10 minutes, until the wine has reduced by about half. Add the water, cover the skillet, and reduce the heat to low. Cook the sprouts for about 20 minutes more, until they are tender and the liquid has evaporated.

Remove the skillet from the stove and place it under the broiler for 3 to 5 minutes, until the sprouts are crisp and slightly toasted.

Remove the skillet from the oven and season the sprouts lightly with salt and pepper. Finish with a sprinkling of cheese and serve immediately.

2 pounds Brussels sprouts, rinsed, ends trimmed

8 ounces thick English pork shoulder bacon, cut into ½-inch pieces

1 large white onion, quartered and cut into ¼-inch-thick strips

1 cup dry white wine

½ cup water

Coarse sea salt

Freshly ground black pepper

Good-quality Parmesan cheese, freshly grated

# Blanquette de Veau

**B**lanquette de Veau—a creamy, white broth–based veal stew—is as French as *bonjour*. There are as many ways to prepare this dish as there are people who make it. I have developed this recipe over the years and find it fits my ideal of a good *blanquette*. The lemon gives the sauce a hint of tang, while earthy overtones from the mushrooms and nutmeg contribute a woodsy flavor. If you prefer, chicken is a good substitute for the classic veal. *(See page 163.)*

Put the veal pieces in a large stockpot and cover them with cold water. Bring the water to a boil over high heat, and let the veal cook in the boiling water for 5 minutes. Remove the pot from the heat and drain the veal in a colander, discarding the water. Rinse the drained veal pieces with cold water, return them to the pot, and add the carrot, onion, leek, bouquet garni, a pinch of salt, and the peppercorns. Pour in the stock and add cold water as needed to cover the ingredients. Bring the liquid to a boil, then cover the pot, reduce the heat to low, and simmer for 1½ hours, or until the vegetables are soft and the veal is cooked through.

Remove the pot from the heat and transfer the meat to a platter. Cover the meat with foil to keep it warm. Discard the vegetables and bouquet garni. Strain the stock through a fine-mesh sieve into another clean stockpot. Cover the pot and keep the strained stock warm over very low heat while you prepare the roux.

In a 3-quart saucepan, melt the butter over medium-low heat, then add the flour, and whisk until bubbly but not brown. Gradually whisk in 1¼ cups of the warm stock, adding more as needed until the mixture is smooth and has the consistency of heavy cream. Rinse out the first stockpot and set it aside.

Add the mushrooms to the thickened roux, and cook gently for 10 minutes. Season to taste with fine sea salt and freshly ground black pepper, and stir in the lemon juice. Remove the pan from the heat.

In a small bowl, mix together the crème fraîche and egg yolk, and then slowly stir the mixture into the mushroom sauce.

In the clean stockpot, combine the sauce with the meat. Adjust the seasonings to taste and stir in the nutmeg. To serve, scoop ½ cup of rice on each individual serving plate and ladle the Blanquette de Veau over the top.

**N O T E :** The remaining stock can be frozen and used for soups or other dishes at a later time.

---

3 pounds trimmed boneless veal shoulder, cut into 2-inch pieces

1 medium carrot

1 medium onion

1 leek, green part removed and discarded

1 bouquet garni of celery, thyme, parsley, and bay leaf (see page 52)

Pinch of coarse sea salt

5 whole black peppercorns

5 cups chicken stock

3 tablespoons unsalted butter, at room temperature

2 tablespoons all-purpose flour

24 small button mushrooms

Freshly ground black pepper

Juice of ½ lemon

½ cup crème fraîche

1 large egg yolk

Dash of freshly grated nutmeg

3 to 4 cups cooked white rice, for serving (about ½ cup per person)

# Tarte Tatin

*Serves 8*

This delicious medley of butter, sugar, and apples was developed by the Tatin sisters in France during the late nineteenth century. I love it served with a good dollop of crème fraîche.

Preheat the oven to 400°F. Place a 10-inch cast-iron skillet over low heat to warm for 5 minutes.

In a heavy-bottomed saucepan, combine the butter and sugar over medium heat, stirring constantly, until the butter melts and the sauce turns a pale golden brown, for 8 to 10 minutes.

Working quickly, pour the sauce into the bottom of the pre-warmed cast-iron skillet and spread it to evenly coat the bottom of the pan.

Arrange the apples in the pan on top of the sauce, cored sides up. Cover the apples with the puff pastry, prick the pastry all over with a fork, and transfer the skillet to the oven. Bake for 40 to 50 minutes, or until the pastry is golden brown.

Remove the skillet from the oven and let it cool for 10 to 15 minutes. Place a serving platter on top of the skillet, and carefully invert the tart. Cut the tart into slices and serve each with a dollop of crème fraîche.

6 tablespoons unsalted butter

1 cup granulated sugar

6 baking apples, peeled, cored, and halved

1 sheet puff pastry, thawed if frozen

Crème fraîche, for serving

# Elegant Christmas Eve Dinner

Sea Salt Chocolate Honey Caramels

Polish Christmas Eve Mushroom Soup

Roasted Goose with Prune and Apple Stuffing

Pommes de Terre Duchesse

Carrots Glacé

Poached Fig and Pear Beggars' Purses

Red Bordeaux

T

HE CHRISTMAS SEASON IS SUCH AN EXCITING TIME of year. There's something special about the hustle and bustle of the season, which makes each task a pleasure—from the decorating to the entertaining and gift giving—and whether Thomas and I are in the country or the city, there are always loads of parties and lots of people to see.

Of all the holiday activities, cooking is the most pleasurable for me. The recipes that I use are traditional ones that have been passed down through the family and tweaked here and there to make them more my own. In our family, the big feast is always on Christmas Eve, and after dessert we open our presents.

Since the bagatelle is like a bijoux, I felt it would be the perfect setting for an end-of-the-year feast. I dressed the garden gate in a beautiful wreath adorned with pomegranates and gold leaves and used the several inches of freshly fallen snow to make a snowman welcoming committee, which greeted guests at the entrance to the garden.

I was inspired to make these little snowmen after a recent snowy trip to Paris. In spite of the fact that I had lived in the City of Lights for several years and have visited countless times since, I had never before witnessed the French fascination for snowmen. All of a sudden, after a heavy snow, the city was transformed into a village of snowmen, which popped up everywhere—from bus stops to the steps of the Bibliothèque Mazarin.

In the bagatelle, I wanted to create a dazzling interior where just about everything glittered and sparkled, even the fabric on the walls. For this dinner, I had my "Celeste" pattern custom-printed in glittery, gold metallic-on-white fine-wale corduroy. A large piece of bright red felt made for a vibrant tablecloth that doubled as a table pad.

The centerpieces were an ode to creativity. A glistening "forest" was made using rock candy, and for a little twinkle, Styrofoam cones were covered in pine and strung with miniature battery-operated lights. Small gold-washed votives were layered throughout the "forest" for additional glimmer.

For the menu, I relied on a mix of favorite dishes, starting with Thomas's family recipe for traditional Polish mushroom soup. For the main course, Roasted Goose with Prune and Apple Stuffing made for a striking presentation, alongside platters of Pommes de Terre Duchesse and Carrots Glacé.

We ended the dinner with Poached Fig and Pear Beggars' Purses. These little gems take a bit of effort but the result is so worth it. They make a memorable end to a special holiday meal.

OPPOSITE: The bagatelle decked out for Christmas Eve dinner. The walls were covered in my "Celeste" pattern, printed in metallic gold on white corduroy and trimmed with a red ribbon. OVERLEAF, LEFT: I used my great-grandmother's Limoges china. The sparkle of the cut Baccarat crystal adds a festive note. The marvelous trees made from rock candy contrast with evergreen trees strung with battery-operated LED lights. OVERLEAF, RIGHT (clockwise from top left): Caramels double as a place card and a gift. Each guest received a small present of an evergreen-scented candle. A hearty mushroom soup. I folded napkins into a Christmas tree shape and adorned them with gold-painted metal oak leaves.

## TIPS

- When making snowmen, if the snow is too dry, spray it with a fine mist of water.

- Although I don't grow lemons or oranges in my garden, I use them regularly in my winter dishes. The citrus peels are great for compost but only if they are from organic fruit.

- Keep the cyclamen plants happy by watering them regularly throughout the winter. The reward will be almost-constant blooms until the end of spring.

RIGHT: On the console I created a family of whimsical snowmen, sporting little "Michael Devine" fabric scarves, to greet guests. Red cyclamen adds color. OVERLEAF, LEFT: The wreath on the garden gate sports pomegranates and gold spray-painted leaves. OVERLEAF, RIGHT: The garden's centerpiece is a wonderful display of greenery and red berries.

# Sea Salt Chocolate Honey Caramels

*Makes 60 caramels*

These caramels combine three of my favorite ingredients: chocolate, fleur de sel, and honey. I packaged them in cellophane bags, tied with red and antique gold ribbons, and used them as place-card holders so my guests could take home delicious reminders of the evening. *(See page 175.)*

Line a 9-by-13-inch rectangular cake pan with parchment paper, butter the paper lightly, and set aside. Cut sixty 3-by-4-inch pieces of parchment or waxed paper, to be used as the caramel wrappers, and set aside.

Combine the chocolate, sugar, honey, vanilla, and butter in a medium nonstick saucepan over low heat and simmer for 10 minutes, or until an instant-read candy thermometer registers 234°F (the soft-ball stage).

Pour the mixture into the prepared cake pan. With an offset metal spatula, spread it into an even layer. Let the caramel stand at room temperature for 1 hour to harden. When the caramel is firm, turn it onto a cutting board and sprinkle to taste with fleur de sel. Using a sharp knife, cut the caramel into sixty 1-inch squares.

Wrap the pieces in the papers, twisting the ends.

4 ounces 60% dark chocolate, coarsely chopped

¼ cup granulated sugar

¾ cup raw honey

1 teaspoon pure vanilla extract

¼ cup (½ stick) unsalted butter

Fleur de sel

# Polish Christmas Eve Mushroom Soup

*Serves 6*

This soup is a Polish dish that is traditionally served at the start of Christmas Eve dinner. It's made with dried Borowik mushrooms. *(See page 175.)*

The day before, put the mushrooms in a mixing bowl and add 3 cups water. Soak overnight at room temperature.

Remove the softened mushrooms from the water and set the bowl and soaking liquid aside. Cut the mushrooms into bite-sized pieces. Strain the soaking liquid into a 3-quart saucepan through a fine sieve lined with cheesecloth. Place the pan over medium heat, and add 5 cups water, along with the vinegar, bouillon cubes, and chopped mushrooms. Simmer the soup for 1 hour, then reduce the heat to low.

Melt the butter in a small saucepan over medium heat. Add the flour and cook, stirring constantly, until the mixture is smooth and uniform in color, 3 to 5 minutes. Remove 1 cup of the soup broth and add it to the butter-flour mixture, whisking constantly until it has thickened and is free of lumps. Stir the thickened mixture into the soup. Cook for an additional 10 minutes to fully incorporate. Taste and add salt if necessary. Ladle the soup into individual bowls.

4 ounces dried Borowik mushrooms (cèpes can be substituted)

1½ tablespoons white vinegar

4 beef bouillon cubes

2 tablespoons unsalted butter

3 tablespoons all-purpose flour

6 sprigs fresh Italian flat-leaf parsley for garnish (optional)

# Pommes de Terre Duchesse

*Serves 6*

Pommes de Terre Duchesse are made following the same basic steps as mashed potatoes, but they are then piped into elegant rounds and baked in the oven until golden brown. Simple yet refined, these "dressed up" mashed potato cakes are perfect for special occasions.

Preheat the oven to 450°F. Line a large baking sheet with parchment paper, and set aside.

Fill a large pot with cold water and add the potatoes and coarse sea salt. Bring the water to a boil over medium-high heat and cook until the potatoes are fork tender, about 20 minutes. Remove the pot from the heat and drain the potatoes in a colander. Transfer the potatoes to a large bowl, mash them with a potato masher until smooth, then pass the potatoes through a fine-mesh sieve into a large saucepan. Place the pan over medium heat and cook the potatoes for 3 to 5 minutes, or until they are dry.

Remove the pan from the heat and season to taste with the fine sea salt, white pepper, and a dash or two of nutmeg, and mix well. Add the butter and mix well with a whisk or a handheld electric mixer. Fold the egg yolks into the potatoes with a silicone spatula.

Spoon the potatoes into a pastry bag fitted with a ½-inch star tip, and pipe the potatoes onto the prepared baking sheet in 3-inch rounds, spacing them about 2 inches apart.

Transfer the baking sheet to the oven, and bake for 10 to 12 minutes or until the potatoes are light golden. Serve immediately.

2 pounds russet potatoes, peeled and quartered

1 tablespoon coarse sea salt

Fine sea salt

Freshly ground white pepper

Freshly grated nutmeg

6 tablespoons unsalted butter

2 large egg yolks

# Carrots Glacé

*Serves 6*

These caramelized carrots are an elegant side dish. Though this French recipe traditionally employs the cutting technique of *tourné*—a method of cutting vegetables into oblong, football-like shapes—I save time by using prepackaged baby carrots.

In a large sauté pan, combine the carrots, butter, and sugar, and pour in enough water to just cover the carrots. Place the pan over high heat and bring the water to a boil, then reduce the heat to medium and simmer for 20 to 25 minutes, stirring gently every few minutes, until the water has evaporated, and the carrots are evenly caramelized.

Remove the pan from the heat and season with salt to taste. Serve immediately.

1 (16-ounce) bag baby carrots

4 tablespoons unsalted butter

3 tablespoons granulated sugar

Fine sea salt

# Roasted Goose with Prune and Apple Stuffing

*Serves 6*

**R**oasted goose is a classic and relatively straightforward holiday main course. However, be prepared for the large quantities of fat rendered during the cooking process. (I save it in a glass jar for use in sautéed or roasted potatoes.)

The day before, combine the tea and the prunes in a medium bowl. Cover and soak the prunes overnight at room temperature.

When you are ready to roast the goose, drain the prunes and place them in a large bowl along with the apples. Toss to combine, then season to taste with salt and pepper.

Preheat the oven to 400°F.

Pour ¼ inch warm water into a roasting pan. (This will prevent the goose fat from smoking and splattering in the oven.) Set a wire rack in the pan.

Rinse the goose inside and out with water and remove any excess fat. Prick the skin lightly with a fork, being careful not to pierce the flesh of the goose. Stuff the cavity with the apple-prune mixture and rub the outside of the goose with the butter.

Place the goose on the rack in the pan, breast side up. Transfer the pan to the oven and roast for about 1 hour, or until the goose is brown on all sides. Do not baste more than once or twice—the natural fat makes the goose self-basting and the skin will be crispier. Remove the pan from the oven and drain the grease into a heatproof container for future use.

Return the goose to the oven, lower the temperature to 350°F, and roast for another 45 minutes, or until the juices run clear and an instant-read thermometer inserted into the thickest part of the breast registers 180°F.

Remove the pan from the oven and transfer the goose to a carving board. Let the goose stand for 20 minutes before carving.

2 cups brewed green tea, cooled

1 pound pitted prunes

2 pounds apples, peeled, cored, and coarsely chopped

Fine sea salt

Freshly ground black pepper

1 fresh (8-pound) goose, giblets removed and discarded (or reserved for another use)

¼ cup (½ stick) unsalted butter, at room temperature

# Poached Fig and Pear Beggars' Purses

*Serves 6*

Ⅰf there is one dessert that is sure to impress, this is it. It takes a bit of time, but the result is outstanding. Most of the pears and figs are poached in a port-and-vanilla sauce before baking, and the rest are caramelized and served alongside the finished dessert.

Combine the orange juice, port, 3/4 cup of the sugar, and the vanilla bean in a 3-quart saucepan. Whisk the mixture until the sugar has dissolved, then set aside.

Peel, quarter, core, and dice 1½ of the pears into uniform ¼-inch cubes. Add the chopped pears to the orange juice–port mixture, and stir to combine. Cover the saucepan, and cook over low heat for 15 minutes, or until the pears have softened a bit but are still firm.

Peel and dice 8 of the figs. Add them to pan, and continue to cook for 10 minutes.

Peel, quarter, and core the remaining pear. Cut each quarter into four slices and add the slices to the pan for 5 minutes to briefly poach them. Remove the slices, and set aside.

Remove the vanilla bean from the fruit mixture, let it cool slightly, and then cut it into six long, thin strips, and set aside.

Drain the fruit in a fine-mesh sieve set over a large bowl, reserving the poaching liquid, and set it aside to cool completely.

Preheat the oven to 425°F. Line a large baking sheet with parchment paper.

Pour the reserved poaching liquid into a small saucepan and bring it to a simmer over low heat. Cook for 15 minutes, or until the liquid is reduced to a thick syrup.

Lightly flour a work surface and place one of the phyllo sheets on top. Brush it lightly with 1 tablespoon of the butter, and fold the sheet in half. Place 1 heaping tablespoon of the fruit mixture in the center of the folded sheet, draw the phyllo up into a purse shape around the fruit, and tie the phyllo closed with a strip of the vanilla bean. Let the purse rest for 2 minutes to stabilize it before moving it with a flat spatula to the prepared baking sheet. Repeat with the remaining sheets of phyllo dough, 5 tablespoons butter, fruit mixture, and vanilla bean strips to make five more purses.

Bake the purses for 15 minutes, or until lightly browned. Remove the baking sheet from the oven, and transfer the purses to a rack to cool.

Meanwhile, cut the remaining 6 figs in half.

Put the remaining ¼ cup sugar in a 10-inch nonstick sauté pan and cook it over medium-high heat until it begins to turn a pale copper color, about 5 minutes. Add the reserved pear slices and the halved figs and sauté them for 1 to 2 minutes,

Juice of 1 orange

5 tablespoons port

1 cup granulated sugar

1 vanilla bean, split and scraped

2½ large just-ripe pears (they should still be firm), divided

14 ripe but firm figs

6 sheets phyllo dough, thawed if frozen

8 tablespoons melted butter

All-purpose flour, for dusting

until they are just caramelized. Add the remaining 2 tablespoons butter to the pan to stop the cooking.

Remove the pan from the heat, transfer the caramelized fruit to a large plate, and set aside.

To serve, place one beggar's purse and two slices of pear and fig on each individual plate, and drizzle with the syrup from the pan.

# Acknowledgments

My gratitude goes to Jessica Napp for opening the door for this book to become a reality. Thanks also to my editor, Sandy Gilbert, whose masterful expertise and vast experience helped shape my vision, and for the support of Rizzoli's publisher, Charles Miers. Thanks to Susi Oberhelman for the brilliant design that brought these pages to life, to Peggy Paul for helping me whip the manuscript into shape, and to John Gruen for his colorful photographs of the bagatelle.

This book would not have been possible without the unwavering help and support of my partner, Thomas Burak.

How can I sufficiently thank my friend and mentor Charlotte Moss, who encouraged the idea and lent her sage advice at every turn? Her support throughout this project means the world to me.

This book took a village to produce. A special thank-you to my friends in Kinderhook, New York: Stuart and Audrey Peckner, whose endless supply of tabletop accessories made many of the shoots perfection; Stuart and Deborah Minton, who helped shape the menus and gave wonderful suggestions; Joanna Giltner, whose boundless enthusiasm was always welcomed; Anne Marie Bankert of Kinderhook Corners, whose iced coffee and cappuccinos kept me going; and Richard Heron, who never turned down a request for help no matter how tedious.

Thanks also to my good friends Ronda Rice Carmen, who is always one step ahead, Sandra Redman, who gave great advice and never failed to lend an ear, and Elizabeth Blitzer, Janet Schlesinger, and Christina Juarez, who introduced me to many vendors and also shared their expertise.

Thanks to the many suppliers who generously loaned objects that are featured in many of the photographs: William Yeoward, Baccarat Crystal, Marie Daâge, Hedstrom & Judd, Vietri, Dransfield and Ross, and especially Mottahedah, Juliska, and Sferra, whose company representatives were patient with my endless requests. And thank you to the Berry Farm of Chatham, who always was there to supply all the Christmas greens and some winter produce I needed to create a festive ending.

A fountain filled with Mme Caroline de Testout roses and petals adds the soft melody of water to the garden's tranquil ambiance.

# Resources

These are my favorite go-to resources for tabletop accessories, linens, garden seeds, fresh greens, and garden plants. They always have the best selections, and the quality is outstanding.

**BACCARAT**
635 Madison Avenue
New York, New York 10022
(212) 826-6533
www.baccarat.com
Top-of-the-line French crystal company.

**THE BERRY FARM**
2309 State Route 203
Chatham, New York 12037
(518) 392-4609
www.thechathamberryfarm.com
A Columbia county mecca for organic produce and plants.

**GILMOR GLASS**
2 Main Street
Millerton, New York 12546
(518) 789-6700
www.gilmorglass.com
A wonderful source for artisanal glassware made on the premises by a master craftsman.

**HEDSTROM & JUDD**
401 Warren Street
Hudson, New York 12534
(518) 671-6131
www.hedstromjudd.com
Swedish design at its best.

**JULISKA**
465 Canal Street
Stamford, Connecticut 06902
(888) 414-8448
www.juliska.com
Great selection of elegant, casual dinnerware, glassware, and flatware.

**KITCHEN GARDEN SEEDS**
23 Tulip Drive (P.O. Box 638)
Bantam, Connecticut 06750
(860) 567-6086
www.kitchengardenseeds.com
My go-to resource for foolproof seeds.

**MARIE DAÂGE**
14, rue Portalis
75008 Paris
(011) 33.1.44.90.01.36
www.mariedaage.com
The finest hand-painted Limoges china in the world, available in a rainbow of colors.

**MICHAEL DEVINE, LTD.**
10 Broad Street
Kinderhook, New York 12106
(646) 912-1032
www.michaeldevinehome.com
Fabrics, china, and accessories for the home made from hand-printed fabrics.

**MOTTAHEDEH**
41 Madison Avenue
New York, New York 10100
(212) 685-3050
www.mottahedeh.com
Amazing collection of chic, traditional dinnerware and accessories.

**NP TRENT ANTIQUES**
555 Warren Street
Hudson, New York 12534
(518) 828-1100
www.nptrentantiques.com
A great source for outstanding one-of-a-kind antiques.

**SFERRA FINE LINENS**
15 Mayfield Avenue
Edison, New Jersey 08837
(732) 225-6290
www.sferra.com
My favorite makers of colorful solid linen napkins in an array of useful sizes.

**VIETRI**
41 Madison Avenue
New York, New York 10100
(919) 732-5933
www.vietri.com
Rustic Italian-influenced designed dinnerware and flatware.

**WILLIAM YEOWARD**
41 Madison Avenue
New York, New York 10100
(212) 532-2358
www.williamyeowardcrystal.com
A wonderful, endless selection of crystal glassware.

## CONVERSION CHARTS

All conversions are approximate.

### WEIGHT CONVERSIONS

| U.S./U.K. | Metric |
|---|---|
| ½ oz | 14 g |
| 1 oz | 28 g |
| 1½ oz | 43 g |
| 2 oz | 57 g |
| 2½ oz | 71 g |
| 3 oz | 85 g |
| 3½ oz | 100 g |
| 4 oz | 113 g |
| 5 oz | 142 g |
| 6 oz | 170 g |
| 7 oz | 200 g |
| 8 oz | 227 g |
| 9 oz | 255 g |
| 10 oz | 284 g |
| 11 oz | 312 g |
| 12 oz | 340 g |
| 13 oz | 368 g |
| 14 oz | 400 g |
| 15 oz | 425 g |
| 1 lb | 454 g |

### LIQUID CONVERSIONS

| U.S. | Metric |
|---|---|
| 1 tsp | 5 ml |
| 1 tbs | 15 ml |
| 2 tbs | 30 ml |
| 3 tbs | 45 ml |
| ¼ cup | 60 ml |
| ⅓ cup | 75 ml |
| ⅓ cup + 1 tbs | 90 ml |
| ⅓ cup + 2 tbs | 100 ml |
| ½ cup | 120 ml |
| ⅔ cup | 150 ml |
| ¾ cup | 180 ml |
| ¾ cup + 2 tbs | 200 ml |
| 1 cup | 240 ml |
| 1 cup + 2 tbs | 275 ml |
| 1¼ cups | 300 ml |
| 1⅓ cups | 325 ml |
| 1½ cups | 350 ml |
| 1⅔ cups | 375 ml |
| 1¾ cups | 400 ml |
| 1¾ cups + 2 tbs | 450 ml |
| 2 cups (1 pint) | 475 ml |
| 2½ cups | 600 ml |
| 3 cups | 720 ml |
| 4 cups (1 quart) | 945 ml |
| (1,000 ml is 1 liter) | |

### OVEN TEMPERATURES

| °F | Gas Mark | °C |
|---|---|---|
| 250 | ½ | 120 |
| 275 | 1 | 140 |
| 300 | 2 | 150 |
| 325 | 3 | 165 |
| 350 | 4 | 180 |
| 375 | 5 | 190 |
| 400 | 6 | 200 |
| 425 | 7 | 220 |
| 450 | 8 | 230 |
| 475 | 9 | 240 |
| 500 | 10 | 260 |
| 550 | Broil | 290 |

The Mottahedah salad plates selected for my Early Autumn Dinner are adorned with botanical illustrations of fall nuts—a hazelnut, pecan, chestnut, and acorn. A ceramic mushroom and a pea knife rest are from France.

Thomas

# Index

## CREDITS

All photographs by Michael Devine, with the exception of the following images that were taken by John Gruen: pages 14, 17, 18, 19, 20, 21, 37, 53, 81, 103, 104, 105 (top left and right, bottom right), 107, 113, 141, 155, 158, 161, 162, 163, 173, 174, 175 (top left and right, bottom left), and 182.

Page 12: Eugène Delacroix's quote from the artist's journal, December 28, 1857, used with the permission of the Musée Eugène Delacroix, Paris, France

First published in the United States of America in 2014
by Rizzoli International Publications, Inc.    |    300 Park Avenue South    |    New York, New York 10010    |    www.rizzoliusa.com

2014 2015 2016 2017 /10 9 8 7 6 5 4 3 2 1    |    Printed in China

ISBN 13: 978-0-8478-4251-3    |    Library of Congress Control Number: 2013953187

Project Editor: Sandra Gilbert
Art Direction: Susi Oberhelman, SVO Graphic Design

ABOVE: Fresh cut lilacs brimming in a vintage galvanized watering can are ready to be used for a flower arrangement. PAGE 1: Mara des Bois strawberries are a bountiful and ever-bearing variety. PAGES 2 AND 3: Vegetable topiaries make a striking centerpiece for my Early Autumn Dinner. PAGE 4: A warm summer afternoon is ideal for savoring lobsters.